AF783139

SUBCOMMITTEE ON LIVESTOCK

HAROLD L. VOLKMER, Missouri, *Chairman*

GARY A. CONDIT, California, *Vice Chairman*
EARL HILLIARD, Alabama
CHARLES W. STENHOLM, Texas
TIM HOLDEN, Pennsylvania
JILL L. LONG, Indiana
COLLIN C. PETERSON, Minnesota
CHARLIE ROSE, North Carolina
CALVIN M. DOOLEY, California
BILL SARPALIUS, Texas

STEVE GUNDERSON, Wisconsin
TOM LEWIS, Florida
ROBERT F. (BOB) SMITH, Oregon
JOHN A. BOEHNER, Ohio
BOB GOODLATTE, Virginia
RICHARD W. POMBO, California
FRANK D. LUCAS, Oklahoma

CONTENTS

H.R. 4744, THE NATIONAL AQUACULTURE DEVELOPMENT, COMMERCIALIZATION, AND PROMOTION ACT OF 1994

TUESDAY, OCTOBER 4, 1994

HOUSE OF REPRESENTATIVES, SUBCOMMITTEE ON DEPARTMENT OPERATIONS AND NUTRITION, JOINT WITH SUBCOMMITTEE ON LIVESTOCK, COMMITTEE ON AGRICULTURE,

Washington, DC.

The subcommittees met, pursuant to call, at 10:15 a.m., in room 1302, Longworth House Office Building, Hon. Charles W. Stenholm (chairman of the Subcommittee on Department Operations and Nutrition) presiding, together with Hon. Harold L. Volkmer (chairman of the Subcommittee on Livestock).

Present for the Subcommittee on Department Operations and Nutrition: Representatives Inslee, Volkmer, Lambert, Gunderson, Allard, and Canady.

Present for the Subcommittee on Livestock: Representatives Volkmer, Stenholm, Gunderson, and Goodlatte.

Staff present: John Frank, deputy minority counsel; Brenda Connolly, clerk; Stan Ray, Timothy P. De Coster, and Pete Thomson.

OPENING STATEMENT OF HON. CHARLES W. STENHOLM, A REPRESENTATIVE IN CONGRESS FROM THE STATE OF TEXAS

Mr. STENHOLM. The subcommittees will come to order.

The legislation before today's joint subcommittee hearing is H.R. 4744, the National Aquaculture Development, Commercialization, and Promotion Act of 1994, introduced in July of this year.

At issue is a rapidly growing industry and the need for support, promotion, and coordination among Federal policies affecting that industry. In considering these issues, there is an increasing interest in extending existing authority and expanding the responsibilities of the Federal Government, particularly the U.S. Department of Agriculture. This legislation represents an effort to address these issues in a comprehensive and noncontroversial manner.

I commend my colleague from Arkansas, Ms. Lambert, for introducing this legislation as a point from which the committee can actively participate in this important debate and look forward to the testimony from our witnesses.

[H.R. 4744 appears at the conclusion of the hearing.]

HON. HAROLD L. VOLKMER, CHAIRMAN

SUBCOMMITTEE ON LIVESTOCK

OPENING REMARKS

THE SUBCOMMITTEE ON LIVESTOCK IS PLEASED TO JOIN THIS MORNING WITH THE DEPARTMENT OPERATIONS AND NUTRITION SUBCOMMITTEE TO REVIEW H.R. 4744, INTRODUCED BY OUR COLLEAGUE, BLANCHE LAMBERT.

I LOOK FORWARD TO LEARNING MORE ABOUT THIS LEGISLATION AND HOW IT WILL FURTHER THE DEVELOPMENT OF THE PROMISING AQUACULTURE INDUSTRY IN THE UNITED STATES, AND WE WILL BE INTERESTED TO HEAR THE ADMINISTRATION'S COMMENTS ON THE BILL.

I COMMEND MS. LAMBERT FOR HER LEADERSHIP IN INTRODUCING THIS MEASURE, AND I LOOK FORWARD TO WORKING WITH HER ON THIS ISSUE IN THE FUTURE.

Mr. STENHOLM. Ms. Lambert.

OPENING STATEMENT OF HON. BLANCHE M. LAMBERT, A REPRESENTATIVE IN CONGRESS FROM THE STATE OF ARKANSAS

Ms. LAMBERT. Thank you, Mr. Chairman. I have a brief opening statement. I would certainly like to thank you and Mr. Volkmer before we begin. I want to express my sincere appreciation to both of you for all of your hard work during the 103d Congress on behalf of all American agriculture.

I particularly want to thank you for taking the time to hold this hearing on H.R. 4744, the National Aquaculture Development, Commercialization, and Promotion Act of 1994. This is a companion to S. 1288, which Senator Akaka of Hawaii introduced last year.

I introduced this bill in the House after an outpouring of support from the fish farmers in my district, as well as from around the country. Aquaculture is the fastest growing segment of U.S. agriculture with farmgate receipts exceeding $800 million in 1991 alone.

Aquaculture is an industry that is truly nationwide, with more than 30 States that produce at least two dozen commercially viable species. In my home State, aquaculture, including catfish and baitfish production, has a $600 million impact on the State's economy.

While these statistics are impressive, there is still an awful lot of room for improvement. The United States currently imports 60 percent of its fish and shellfish resulting in a $3.3 billion annual trade deficit for seafood. We have seen unprecedented attention given to trade issues, including the expansion of the markets for American products. I believe that we have the opportunity to assist U.S. aquaculture in gaining a greater global market share creating jobs in rural America, and I believe this is just the bill that will help us do this.

H.R. 4744 will help strengthen U.S. aquaculture by utilizing the resources that have made our land-based agriculture so successful. The bill declares private aquaculture to be a form of agriculture and designates USDA as the lead agency for aquaculture.

The bill also authorizes the Secretary of Agriculture to make grants to support applied research and new products that have the best chance for commercial development.

In addition, H.R. 4744 will make fish farmers eligible for disaster assistance as well as farm credit.

I thank you, Chairman Stenholm and Chairman Volkmer, for your support and I look forward to today's testimony.

I yield back the balance of my time.

Mr. STENHOLM. Mr. Volkmer.

Mr. VOLKMER. Mr. Chairman, I have an opening statement I would like to be inserted in the record immediately following your opening statement.

[The prepared statement of Mr. Volkmer follows Mr. Stenholm's opening statement.]

Mr. STENHOLM. Without objection.

Mr. Mr. Goodlatte.

Mr. GOODLATTE. I do not have an opening statement, Mr. Chairman.

Mr. STENHOLM. Any prepared statements received from the members will be placed at this point in the record.

[The prepared statement of Mr. Emerson follows:]

BILL EMERSON
MEMBER OF CONGRESS
8TH DISTRICT, MISSOURI

HOUSE COMMITTEE ON AGRICULTURE
HOUSE COMMITTEE ON PUBLIC WORKS AND TRANSPORTATION

Congress of the United States
House of Representatives
Washington, DC 20515-2508

OFFICES:
SUITE 2454
RAYBURN BUILDING
WASHINGTON, DC 20515-2508
202/225-4404

THE FEDERAL BUILDING
339 BROADWAY
CAPE GIRARDEAU, MO 63701
314/335-0101

612 PINE
ROLLA, MO 65401
314/364-2455

STATEMENT OF CONGRESSMAN BILL EMERSON
BEFORE THE DEPARTMENT OPERATIONS
AND NUTRITION SUBCOMMITTEE
OCTOBER 4, 1994

Mr. Chairman, I wish to thank you and our ranking Member, Mr. Robert Smith, for holding this important forum on an agricultural issue growing in importance throughout the Mississippi Delta region.

There was once a time when fish farming simply entailed pulling a catfish out of the local lake or creek on a sunny afternoon with your favorite fishing pole in hand. Today, catfish farming and the food production of many fish and shellfish have become a full-time industry growing by leaps and bounds. This growth hasn't been easy, but the potential benefits to rural America are tremendous.

I believe the U.S. Department of Agriculture needs to play a role in sustaining this industry's progress through this measure which I strongly support -- H.R. 4744, the National Aquaculture Development, Commercialization, and Promotion Act of 1994. This measure will establish a comprehensive federal policy to promote and encourage the successful establishment of the American aquacultural livelihood.

American aquaculture is giving new hope to farmers looking for new agricultural alternatives. Besides providing a new and profitable alternative crop, aquaculture has helped reduce our national balance-of-payment deficit by increasing consumption of domestically produced seafood products. Equally important, a burgeoning aquaculture industry has aided rural economic development efforts by creating employment and income opportunities in many of our local towns and communities.

U.S. aquaculture production of edible and inedible fish and shellfish has been on the rise for several years. Helping spark this increase has been the efforts of our nation's catfish operations, many of which are located in Southern Missouri. Technological advances also hold significant promise for the economics of producing fish throughout the Mid-South. Continuing changes such as improvements in hatchery practices, better and more specific feeds, and more efficient oxygen delivery systems are key to helping fish growers increase their level of productivity.

Although aquaculture is still a relatively young industry, its promise for the future is looking very bright. Many challenging production hurdles lie ahead, but the mechanics for the expansion of the domestic aquaculture industry are taking shape. I have complete confidence that the fish farmers of this nation will continue to rise to meet the consumer demands of tommorrow and I look forward to working closely with these producers in the future development of this dynamic, new and promising industry.

Mr. STENHOLM. I call our first witness, Dr. Hank Parker, Director, Office of Aquaculture, Cooperative State Research Service.

Dr. Parker.

STATEMENT OF HENRY S. PARKER, DIRECTOR, OFFICE OF AQUACULTURE, COOPERATIVE STATE RESEARCH SERVICE, U.S. DEPARTMENT OF AGRICULTURE

Mr. PARKER. Thank you, Mr. Chairman, and members of the subcommittees. I appreciate the opportunity to present testimony on behalf of the Department of Agriculture on H.R. 4744, the National Aquaculture Development, Commercialization, and Promotion Act of 1994. My testimony is on behalf of the Department of Agriculture.

Aquaculture will be a major global agricultural growth industry in the 21st century. The United States has an important opportunity to develop an internationally competitive aquaculture industry to serve national needs and the global marketplace. Currently, the United States ranks only 10th in the world in the value of its aquaculture industry, and imports over 60 percent of its seafood from other countries.

Mr. Chairman, I would like to comment briefly on the bill. In the interest of time, I will read highlights from the written testimony that was prepared by the Department of Agriculture in consultation with OMB. I was advised late yesterday by OMB that not all Federal agencies have had time to fully review this testimony.

H.R. 4744 would amend and reauthorize the National Aquaculture Act of 1980. The bill would strengthen and broaden USDA's leadership role in support of private aquaculture by designating USDA as "the lead Federal agency for the development, implementation, promotion, and coordination of national policy and programs for private aquaculture * * *."

The Department recognizes that H.R. 4744 is a bill for private, commercial aquaculture. The Secretary is committed to strong departmental leadership of collaborative interagency programs to support the private U.S. aquaculture industry.

The Department recognizes that aquaculture is an important growing segment of U.S. agriculture that has great potential for jobs creation, rural economies, reduction of the trade deficit, and supplying nutritious, healthful food for the U.S. consumers.

The bill would enable the Secretary of Agriculture to provide a stronger Federal leadership role through the Joint Subcommittee on Aquaculture, the JSA, which has become an effective influential interagency coordinating body. The Secretary welcomes the opportunity to continue to provide strong leadership to this body.

The Department also recognizes that other agencies have programs and interests that can support both private and public aquaculture. However, effective leadership by the Department of Agriculture can promote the continued development of a healthy aquatic farming industry by facilitating cooperation among these agencies.

The Department has several recommendations in the written testimony for minor changes in the bill's language to foster cooperation and collaboration with other agencies. The bill would promote private aquaculture by, "establishing private aquaculture as a form of agriculture and establishing cultivated aquatic animals, plants, microorganisms and their products, produced by private persons and moving in standard commodity channels as agricultural livestock crops, and commodities."

The Department recognizes that private commercial aquaculture is an important growing form of agriculture. The Department is committed to providing a broad range of services for this industry. For example, the Department wishes to work closely with the industry to provide a full range of health services for cultivated aquatic animals. The Department notes that H.R. 4744 would retain section 11 of the National Aquaculture Act, which would specify that nothing in this act shall be construed to amend, repeal, or otherwise modify the authority of any Federal officer, Department, or agency to perform any function, responsibility, or activity authorized under any other provision of law. The Department concurs with this provision.

The bill would establish the Secretary of Agriculture, in consultation with the Secretaries of Commerce and Interior, and other Federal agency heads, to coordinate and implement a national policy for private aquaculture and to modify and update the national aquaculture development plan.

The Department concurs that the Secretary should provide leadership in the development, coordination, and implementation of a national policy for private, commercial aquaculture.

The Department also recognizes that the national aquaculture development plan addresses both private and public aquaculture. The Department concurs that the plan should be revised in collaboration with the Secretaries of Commerce and Interior, and the heads of other agencies as appropriate.

The Department does believe that the provision in the bill specifying that the Secretary shall be responsible for resolving any interagency conflict would infringe upon the discretion of the executive branch to resolve interagencies issues.

The bill would continue authorization for the National Aquaculture Information Center and would expand its responsibilities. The center is an important resource for the U.S. aquaculture community and for the JSA.

The bill would authorize the Secretary to develop and implement an aquaculture commercialization program. The Department agrees that there is a need to support activities that can accelerate the transfer to the marketplace of promising aquaculture research and technologies.

Section 9 of the bill would authorize development of a program by the Administrator of the Environmental Protection Agency, in collaboration with the Secretary of Agriculture, to carry out collaborative interagency programs that demonstrate the application of aquaculture to environmental enhancement and assessment. The Department supports programs that can demonstrate the compatibility of agricultural activities, including aquaculture, with responsible environmental stewardship.

The Department of Agriculture finds that the proposed legislation would apply broadly to the U.S. aquaculture industry, and would strengthen the Department's ability to support cultivation of a wide variety of aquatic species in diverse freshwater and marine environments throughout the United States. The legislation should be an important stimulus to the development of a globally competitive U.S. aquaculture industry. The Department welcomes the opportunity to provide needed assistance to this important developing industry.

Mr. Chairman, this concludes my prepared statement. I will be pleased to respond to any questions.

[The prepared statement of Mr. Parker appears at the conclusion of the hearing.]

Mr. STENHOLM. I believe if I followed you, what is your position on this legislation?

Mr. PARKER. The administration's position on this legislation has not been firmed up yet, Mr. Chairman.

Mr. STENHOLM. I sense from your statements that you find a lot that you do support, but there are some questions and there would be some need for amendment in order to gain the administration's support of this legislation?

Mr. PARKER. Yes, sir. The statements that I read reflect the testimony that has been prepared by the Department of Agriculture.

Mr. STENHOLM. Under the current method of handling aquaculture, would you elaborate a little bit more as to how the various agencies coordinate your activities regarding aquaculture?

Mr. PARKER. The Federal agencies are coordinated through the Joint Subcommittee on Aquaculture. That is the Federal interagency body which is responsible under the National Aquaculture Act for coordination of Federal programs.

The JSA reports to the National Science and Technology Council and the Office of Science and Technology Policy. The JSA is permanently chaired by the Secretary of Agriculture, based on the National Aquaculture Act.

Mr. STENHOLM. Do you have a cost estimate for this legislation?

Mr. PARKER. We do not have a cost estimate, Mr. Chairman. We do not see anything in the legislation that would indicate costs at this point.

Mr. STENHOLM. I believe there are some disaster provisions in the legislation that might entail some costs.

Mr. PARKER. We don't have an estimate of what that would be.

Mr. STENHOLM. In order to provide aquatic animal health programs, does the Department of Agriculture need explicit authority to do so?

Mr. PARKER. Yes. It is the position of the Animal and Plant Health Inspection Service that they do need explicit authority in order to provide those services.

Mr. STENHOLM. And do not have it today?

Mr. PARKER. They do not have what they believe they need.

Mr. STENHOLM. No further questions at this time.

Mr. Volkmer.

Mr. VOLKMER. Thank you. I would like to clear up in my mind what I view as your comments here today have meant is that this bill, to me, needs additional study. In other words, there are some things that you object to, but there are not things that cannot be overcome?

Mr. PARKER. From the prepared statement reflecting the testimony that was developed by the Department of Agriculture, we have made a couple of recommendations that we believe would strengthen the bill. However, as the statement indicated, there are other Federal agencies that have not had adequate time to review it.

Mr. VOLKMER. Right. And those things need to be worked out. In fact, you mentioned that basically this would be a good bill for the 104th Congress.

Mr. PARKER. In the written statement, yes, sir, that is true.

Mr. VOLKMER. Thank you.

Mr. STENHOLM. Ms. Lambert.

Ms. LAMBERT. Thank you, Mr. Chairman.

Dr. Parker, I understand certainly that OMB is sometimes slow to sign off on proposals. This lack of commitment today is not surprising. However, I do want to be clear as well as to what USDA's position is.

We do understand that Commerce and Interior do have a role to play in this. You are indicating that USDA recognizes that, and recognizes that they have not made a statement or come out with a position on the bill.

But you are telling us that the support of USDA hinges on what those other two agencies have to say?

Mr. PARKER. What I am saying is that—and this is my understanding of how the process works—any administration position that is cleared by the administration has to take into account the comments of other Federal agencies. And unless and until that clearance occurs, I am certainly not at liberty to presume what the administration's position would be.

And so what I have presented here is what I can present at this time based on the testimony that came out of the Department of Agriculture.

Ms. LAMBERT. But you can say that USDA, in essence, supports the bill or the concepts that it embodies?

Mr. PARKER. The USDA is committed to leadership of a national aquaculture industry, private commercial aquaculture, is very anxious to work with all agencies in the development of this industry and to provide the kind of leadership that is vested in the Department.

Ms. LAMBERT. Do you feel that this bill would support USDA in their capability to support the U.S. aquaculture industry?

Mr. PARKER. In my personal opinion, yes, I do.

Ms. LAMBERT. I know that we mentioned about the Joint Subcommittee on Aquaculture. Could you just generally sum up for me the activities that you at USDA and the Joint Subcommittee on Aquaculture are working on currently?

Mr. PARKER. We have a major effort underway right now to develop a Federal strategic plan for aquaculture that looks at a variety of research and development opportunities in aquaculture and the roles that the various agencies can play in those research and development activities.

So we are working with the Departments of Commerce and Interior, and a number of other Federal agencies to identify the various roles that those agencies can bring to this.

Ms. LAMBERT. Would this bill enhance your opportunity or your ability to be able to do that?

Mr. PARKER. In my opinion, it would.

Ms. LAMBERT. Why?

Mr. PARKER. Because, in my opinion, I do believe that the Department of Agriculture is an appropriate agency to provide leadership in this area because aquaculture is a form of agriculture. That is my personal opinion.

Ms. LAMBERT. Thank you. No further questions, Mr. Chairman. Thank you.

Mr. STENHOLM. No further questions at this time. I would hope, Dr. Parker—my instructions to our staff will be, upon conclusion of the hearing today, is to see if we can sit down and reach an accommodation or an agreement on this legislation that would have the support of the administration and would have the support of the committee.

And if we can do that, it would be my intent to schedule a markup in subcommittee to see, since I understand there is some considerable support in the other body for this legislation, if it might be possible to find an agreement; but I think we all recognize the lateness of the hour and the day.

But if I gathered from the tenor of your testimony today, you do recognize a need for the legislation. I think it is important that we bring aquaculture into a full standing within the Department of Agriculture. I totally concur with your response to Ms. Lambert and her question that this is very important as we look to the future of a very important industry that has some unique problems today, that they deserve to be a full partner in the agricultural community.

I also recognize we still have a lot of loose ends regarding the reorganization of USDA, and I think it is a very good time for us to seriously look at where aquaculture is going to fit within the reorganization and also within the spirit and framework of the coordination with other agencies, both of the Federal Government and also within the Congress itself.

So this is not a simple task that we set out to do, but it is a very important one, and we thank you for being here this morning and for your testimony. We look forward to working with you.

Mr. PARKER. I would like to add one thing, somewhat in defense of OMB. In August, OMB organized a meeting among three agencies—Department of Commerce, Department of Interior, and the Department of Agriculture—to address some of the issues that were still unresolved on S. 1288 and the Department's report. And I attended that meeting, and I was very encouraged at the meeting of the minds that developed from that.

I felt we were very close to an agreement on the basic principles of legislation. And in drafting this particular testimony, I tried to address that agreement as best I could.

Mr. STENHOLM. Ms. Lambert.

Ms. LAMBERT. Thank you, Mr. Chairman. I would like to thank Dr. Parker for his patience today and his willingness to be a part of this. He did touch on one aspect that I wanted to mention and that was the health aspect.

As we look at health care reform and we talk about the preventive care, we have looked at aquaculture and what it avails as to providing a more abundant, safe and obviously healthy food supply

87-941 O - 95 - 2

as well that we could produce within our own borders as opposed to the importation that we have seen a lot of.

I would like to thank you for bringing to the table where USDA is and I would like to pledge my support as well as my hard work in the next several days. If there is a possibility to work with the other agencies, I would pledge my support and my willingness to work with those agencies along with you to resolve any of the outstanding issues that may be there because we do see a tremendous amount of support not only in our districts but also from up here as well.

We thank you for coming today and we will be glad to work with you.

Mr. STENHOLM. Having observed the lady from Arkansas in previous endeavors when she offers her full support, I suggest the next day or two are going to be very interesting.

Thank you.

Mr. PARKER. Thank you.

Mr. STENHOLM. We will call panel 2: Mr. McCraren, Mr. Zimmerman, Mr. Martin, and Mr. Dorey.

Mr. McCraren.

STATEMENT OF JOSEPH P. McCRAREN, EXECUTIVE DIRECTOR, NATIONAL AQUACULTURE ASSOCIATION, ACCOMPANIED BY TIM MOORE, DIRECTOR, CONGRESSIONAL AFFAIRS

Mr. MCCRAREN. Good morning, Mr. Chairman, and Congresswoman Lambert. I am Joseph McCraren, executive director of the National Aquaculture Association. I wish to thank you for providing me personally, my colleagues, and our industry with the opportunity to speak in support of H.R. 4744, the National Aquaculture Development, Commercialization, and Promotion Act of 1994.

Today, I am speaking on behalf of all members of the National Aquaculture Association. NAA is the youngest and largest aquaculture association in the United States. It is a grassroots, producer-driven, nonprofit organization dedicated to the establishment of policies that further the common interest of its membership, both as individual producers and as members of an industry. NAA currently serves 35 diverse national and State associations whose members produce a variety of species including trout, salmon, catfish, ornamentals, and shellfish.

An analysis by the U.S. Department of Agriculture reveals that aquaculture production in 1980 was 203 million pounds with a farmgate value of $192 million. During the 1980's, production quadrupled, reaching an estimated 860 million pounds, with a farmgate value of more than $760 million by 1990. Aquaculture is a growth industry as evidenced by these data.

Our Nation's aquaculture producers range in size and complexity from corporations employing several hundred workers to small, family-owned farms, commonly referred to as mom and pop operations. They farm a variety of finfish, crustaceans such as crawfish and shrimp, shellfish and aquatic plants. The industry is supported by an infrastructure of feed mills, processing plants, equipment manufacturers and suppliers.

The U.S. industry and its support services account for nearly 300,000 full-time jobs, with a direct and indirect economic impact of $8 billion. And too, aquaculture supplies substantial quantities of finfish for the recreational fishery, which is often overlooked, I might add.

The potential for this industry, the fastest growing segment of agriculture in this country, is vast. Growth would mean jobs and opportunity to many Americans particularly to those in our rural areas. It would provide farmers involved in traditional agriculture with a viable alternative.

Aquaculture currently accounts for less than 9 percent of U.S. seafood production compared to a world average of 16 percent. In 1990, the United States ranked 10th in world aquaculture production.

Aquaculture will be a major global growth industry of the 21st century. According to current projections, based on anticipated population growth and stable or declining capture fisheries harvest, aquaculture production will have to increase sevenfold to supply the world's demand for seafood by the year 2025.

With national commitment and proper planning and support, the United States can realize a major opportunity to develop an important new agricultural industry to serve national needs and the global marketplace. Without such a commitment, the United States will continue to depend on imported fish and shellfish, which now supply over 60 percent of our seafood needs.

Fisheries imports, some $9 billion annually constitute the third largest component of the U.S. trade deficit after petroleum and automobiles. Realization of this legislation will contribute significantly and dramatically to the future of our industry and its meaningfulness to our economy. We appreciate the fact that the bill is of value to all segments of the industry and that it addresses a litany of rudimentary needs necessary for this industry's future.

These include reauthorization of the National Aquaculture Act of 1980, provision for the coordination and implementation of a national aquaculture policy for private industry by the Secretary of Agriculture in consultation with the Secretary of Commerce and Interior, and others as appropriate. We support USDA as lead agency since aquaculture is recognized as agriculture worldwide and should be viewed no differently in our Nation.

Further, cultured aquatic plants and animals would be treated as livestock and agricultural commodities. This is important as it relates to programs of the Department of Agriculture and industry. Important, as well, is reference to a departmental aquacultural plan. We need a departmental focus and infrastructure sensitive to this industry, with a budget reflective of those needs.

We applaud the innovative section on aquaculture commercialization research, revision of the national aquaculture development plan, the bill's facilitation of improved communication and interaction between private industry, Federal Government, and others who make up this diverse community.

We are pleased, as well, with the all-inclusive reference to disaster assistance and certainly the opportunities that farm credit assistance would provide.

It is our hope that we have conveyed in these few minutes the need for this legislation to the subcommittees. We need this bill and we urge the House to support its passage. Our sincere thanks to the subcommittees for agreeing to hold this hearing and to Congresswoman Lambert, her staff and the original cosponsors for developing and introducing this valuable legislation.

I would be pleased to respond to any questions you might have.

[The prepared statement of Mr. McCraren appears at the conclusion of the hearing.]

Mr. STENHOLM. Thank you. Next, Mr. James Zimmerman.

STATEMENT OF JAMES R. ZIMMERMAN, DIRECTOR, PUBLIC RELATIONS, TROUTLODGE, INC., ON BEHALF OF THE WASHINGTON FISH GROWERS ASSOCIATION

Mr. ZIMMERMAN. Thank you, Mr. Chairman, and members of the subcommittees. I am Jim Zimmerman and I represent the Washington Fish Growers Association and my parent company Troutlodge, Incorporated.

In our State, we have 60 fish farmers and we produce 44 million dollars' worth of product. Troutlodge is the largest producer of rainbow trout eggs in the world. We shipped 300 million eggs to 30 States in the Union and 25 foreign countries. We have seven hatcheries, six in Washington and one in Oregon, and we are in five congressional districts. The largest facilities of Troutlodge are located in Congressman Inslee's district, which we stocked 200,000 fish for public catching in his district.

We would like to extend our appreciation to Ms. Lambert for sponsoring this bill. We recognize that it is a form of leadership and we would encourage other Members of Congress to take her bold step to support aquaculture as agriculture.

The important sections of this bill to us out in the State of Washington is definitions. It does create a definition that aquaculture is agriculture. It does create the definition that the Department of Agriculture is the lead agency and it defines our aquatic animals as livestock. This is a critically important definition to those of us who ship across State lines and across international borders.

With that definition, we can rely upon the services of the Animal and Plant Health Inspection Service of the USDA. They are recognized throughout the world for their services and for their professional abilities. We need that service in order to ship our product. I don't know how I can emphasize this more, but if we don't have those services, we don't have a product that we can move. And a nonmovable product is an unsalable product. And although rainbow trout is a marvelous fish, you can only eat so much of it at home.

Mr. Chairmen and members of the subcommittees, I would like to wave another flag. There is no doubt that the industry is agriculture. Those fish belong to us and, with that definition of agriculture and definition of livestock, we can expand into other services and important areas.

It makes us a bankable industry. Right now we are neither fish nor fowl, no pun intended. When we go to a banker, do you go to an agricultural loan officer or do you go to the widget or gadget or what part of the banks industry do we fit? For years we have been recognized as agriculture by the IRS. We need to be bankable in our own communities and, by being defined as agriculture, which this bill, H.R. 4744 and Senator Akaka's bill, S. 1288 does. It takes us into the century that we are headed to as farmers. That is what we are.

I don't know how many pounds of fish are produced by all these other agencies like OMB, but if they need some sort of description, they are welcome to come visit us. We produce a lot of pounds of fish.

Mr. Chairman, with that, I am sure there are other speakers here who can give you more technical details about this bill. But coming from a farmer's point of view, we want to be recognized as a farmer. Everyone else recognizes us as that.

And, again, we thank you for this hearing. And Ms. Lambert and members of this committee, I hope that during your markup session, which comes very soon, that this bill moves along. Thank you.

[The prepared statement of Mr. Zimmerman appears at the conclusion of the hearing.]

Mr. STENHOLM. Thank you. Next, Mr. Martin.

STATEMENT OF ROY MARTIN, EXECUTIVE DIRECTOR, NATIONAL AQUACULTURE COUNCIL, AND VICE PRESIDENT, NATIONAL FISHERIES INSTITUTE

Mr. MARTIN. I would like to take this opportunity to thank Congressman Stenholm and members of both the House Agriculture Subcommittee on Department Operations and Nutrition, and the Subcommittee on Livestock for this invitation to address this most important piece of legislation.

My name is Roy Martin. I am the executive director of the National Aquaculture Council and vice president of the National Fisheries Institute. The council and institute represent over 1,000 companies engaged in all the many aspects of seafood production, marketing, and distribution.

We sincerely appreciate Congresswoman Lambert's interest in the U.S. aquaculture industry and the development of H.R. 4744. The National Aquaculture Council fully supports the intent of H.R. 4744. The council agrees that aquaculture needs the support of the elements contained in this bill.

This whole subject is something that goes beyond committee jurisdiction. This is an issue for the country.

If the Congress and the administration are really serious about aquaculture, and I believe the Congress is, then the following facts and needs should not be denied.

To no one's surprise, the private aquaculture industry is diverse but growing faster than any other segment of agriculture. That is a great start. We now estimate that we employ 300,000 people in actual and related jobs. What kind of job? Rural jobs. That is another positive on our part.

U.S. population rose again last year, but so did total U.S. consumption of seafood. Wild stocks are on the decline. Those stocks need a rest. What will fill the continued demand? Aquaculture could with proper support. No one questions the need for the nutritional benefits that accompany the consumption of seafood.

We—this industry—are the first protectors of water quality, not the EPA. We need an aquaculture policy for the United States.

Where does the leadership really stand on this issue? Aquaculture, no matter how you define it, is husbandry, farming, ranching, livestock, animal health. In other words, agriculture.

The word "aquaculture" needs a leader, a leader that can coordinate its various interpretations by other committees and Departments of Government. In our opinion, USDA is that leader. To maintain this pattern of growth, we will need highly focused research, development, and technology transfer programs, all the elements that are included in this legislation.

We have a national resource that is begging for support; the aquaculture library. We must support the educational aspects of this bill, and without that library support, educational information will not be readily available for our new, future generations of aquaculturists or business leaders in the agriculture community.

Disaster assistance is a needed part of this bill and we support it.

As I have said in previous Senate testimony, I am struck by the opportunities given to jobs and rural development by this industry as I travel the farms, processing plants, and the small towns of America and meet those down-home folks that are U.S. aquaculture. We need action, not more words.

In closing, I would like to thank the subcommittees for this opportunity to present our views on H.R. 4744.

[The prepared statement of Mr. Martin appears at the conclusion of the hearing:]

Mr. STENHOLM. Thank you. Next, Mr. Dorey.

STATEMENT OF CARLTON DOREY, PRODUCER, BRIGHTWATER FARMS, HUMPHREY, AR

Mr. DOREY. Thank you Chairman Stenholm, and Congresswoman Lambert and other honorable members of the Subcommittee. I am Carlton Dorey of Brightwater Farms from Arkansas' First Congressional District. I am a catfish farmer and processor who would like to testify to you concerning the importance of the National Aquaculture Development, Commercialization, and Promotion Act of 1994, H.R. 4744, to my industry.

This bill establishes USDA as the lead agency for aquaculture, which I feel is the correct thing to do because, after all, aquaculture is agriculture.

With USDA as our lead agency, the aquaculture industry will be able to secure a national policy for aquaculture instead of a national strategy. This will enable aquaculture to be included and recognized in all Federal farm programs. My industry is not looking for special treatment by the Federal Government, we just want to be treated the same as other farmers.

Natural disasters strike our farms too and fish farmers should be eligible for farm credit loans and disaster assistance.

This bill states that the Secretary of Agriculture will be the permanent chairperson of the Joint Subcommittee on Aquaculture. Currently, this chair is rotated between the Secretaries of Agriculture, Commerce, and Interior. It is imperative that the Secretary of Agriculture permanently chair this subcommittee to ensure continuity in our national aquaculture policy.

We are like a ship with three captains that all want to steer us in a different policy port. The aquaculture industry in the United States needs a sense of direction from the Federal Government. Our industry will continue to be regulated by numerous Federal agencies, but we need a single agency for guidance and assistance.

As a young industry, our research needs are great and our research dollars are limited. This bill will coordinate our research efforts so that these limited dollars will not be wasted on duplicated research.

I know that other aquaculture bills have been introduced into the House of Representatives, but this bill has truly been written with industry input and only it addresses the issue of a single lead agency.

As you have heard many times, aquaculture is one of the fastest growing segments of the agriculture economy, even with our current fragmented national strategy. Just think of our potential growth and ability to help reduce the national balance of payment deficit once this bill is enacted.

Aquaculture is providing job opportunities in our rural areas, and is providing an area of diversification for existing traditional farms that will enable them to be more profitable. This is a good bill, it has wide industry support, and I urge you to act favorably upon this bill.

Thank you, Mr. Chairman.

[The prepared statement of Mr. Dorey appears at the conclusion of the hearing.]

Mr. STENHOLM. Thank you. I thank each of you.

Ms. Lambert.

Ms. LAMBERT. Thank you, Mr. Chairman.

Just a couple of comments. Mr. Martin did bring up the technology transfer aspect of it and the need for it in the industry. I certainly have been pleased with the partnership that has been forged thus far between USDA and the Department of Energy in their technology transfer programs within their DOE labs.

We have seen some tremendous evidence of ways that they can be helpful, from more effectively oxygenating the water to developing more productive yields and harvesting methods, whether it is sonar or electrification or other methods. But it has been a wonderful experience to see how we can better utilize our Federal dollars, and as they reach out to other industry and provide that technology transfer. It has been a good marriage between agencies and we would like to see that continue, not only with aquaculture but with a multitude of different areas that the technology transfer can bring to us.

And just as Mr. Zimmerman mentioned, there is just so much fish you can eat at home. My husband and I live on a small lake right off the Mississippi and we love to fish. And there is just so much fish you can eat, but it beats the heck out of going to the grocery store. So I always put my pole in the water because I don't much enjoy going to the grocery store.

But the point that you brought up, coming from a seven generation farmer, it is important where we are going with agriculture in this Nation that we do recognize the aquaculture farmer as a bona fide American farmer. It is a very important step in giving them the credibility that they need within the Department of Agriculture as well as within the international marketplace of the support of the agricultural industry in this Nation.

My interest goes back to when I was a little bitty girl and having to be pulled out of a minnow tank at the local bait shop. I got real interested in that venture.

As we look at the characterization of the aquaculture industry and its support for this bill, I would like to hear from any of you all how you characterize the industry's support for the bill, and has the industry changed in any way since the introduction of Senator Akaka's bill over a year ago? I am basically looking for the ideas of what has happened in the industry.

We have seen the recent rice federation coming together, the producers as well as the millers, coming together in aspects that have been very productive, I think, for the rice industry, but to indicate to us some type of mobilization within the industry.

Mr. McCraren. We continue to see great support for your legislation, as well as Senator Akaka's. NAA represents over 2,000 members. There isn't one of them that isn't certainly favorable toward this legislation.

If we have seen anything in terms of change, I would characterize it as a very positive thing, this being with regard to a national aquaculture industry forum that is comprised of industry members. They as well are very supportive and have become quite active themselves recently. So we continue to see nothing but very positive things with regard to this.

Mr. Martin. I have never really seen the seafood industry in total pulling together to bring both the marine side and the land side together in bringing this nutritious product to the consumer. This has never happened before. And aquaculture is that drawing thread bringing that all together. So I think we are on a very positive track here.

Ms. Lambert. That is great.

Mr. Zimmerman. 1995 marks the 50th year of Troutlodge that we have been in business in my State. In 1985, we passed a bill in our State legislature placing aquaculture into the Department of Agriculture. Since 1985, I have been on a number of panels like this, and this year really marks the best year that I have seen in unity.

And I again credit Senator Akaka and yourself for sponsoring these bills which kind of brings to mind that there are now 48 sponsors for S. 1288 in the Senate. So it also shows that the industry is busily informing their Representatives and Senators of the importance of these two pieces of legislation.

Thank you.

Ms. Lambert. Thank you. What do any of you all believe to be the most important provision in the legislation that will actually assist in developing and promoting the aquaculture industry? Are there any specifics?

Mr. Zimmerman. I think we would like to do this from left to right in unison and as loud as we can trumpet it, and that is that the U.S. Department of Agriculture is the lead agency. It makes us a farmer. We are part of the American food suppliers. And that is the business that we are in.

Mr. McCRAREN. I would echo that. With regard to USDA, lead agency as well as reauthorization of the National Aquaculture Act, per se. It is the only piece of legislation that this industry has.

Beyond that, the idea of legitimacy for this industry is extremely appealing. They have been waiting a long time. Thank you.

Mr. DOREY. I would just like to say we would like to see this. This industry needs some stability, and I believe this is going in the right direction.

Mr. MARTIN. To keep our young people on the farm, we need those educational efforts that this bill will provide. To reach backwards and have them vocationally taught aquaculture practices so we can keep those young folks back in agriculture.

Ms. LAMBERT. That sounds good to me. I am for that.

As we talk about what the bill means to the aquaculture in support of that industry, what other kind of support does it lend also to this bill or this bill lends to traditional agriculture? I know that there are other parts of agriculture that obviously support the aquaculture industry and it would be interesting to know if you all, and certainly Mr. Dorey as a producer, you would know as far as the seed and other things or the feed mill that you use and other things, how that would support other aspects of agriculture.

Mr. DOREY. I think this gives us stability in the area of joining this thing together where our financial aspects of the whole aquaculture industry—we as a group, when we go to the lending institutions we are kind of looked at—they don't know who we are when we go in. I think this kind of ties all of us together as an industry, along with other meats as they are. And I think it is a good start for us to tie this together.

Mr. McCRAREN. Certainly the continued utilization of our grains and the like, in our fish feeds.

Mr. ZIMMERMAN. Aquaculture would also be recognized as a minor crop in a whole panoply of events concerning the use of drugs and chemicals. Aquaculture would play an important role there with their counterparts of other forms of agriculture.

The other thing is, we bring an environmental view to the farming in general. And that is, we grow the indicator of clean water, and in our State, we work very closely with neighboring farmers and particularly the potato growers, the corn growers, and the cattlemen of our area. We are surrounded by them at Troutlodge, by all those kinds of farmers, and we work very closely together so that we are all three or all four, if you will, environmentally sound.

Ms. LAMBERT. Mr. Chairman, I yield back the balance of my time.

Mr. STENHOLM. Mr. Zimmerman, I am real curious as to how you can put out 200,000 fish into a stream and some of your other folks out there can do that and I can go fishing and I can't catch a cotton picking one of them. Would you explain that to me?

Mr. ZIMMERMAN. Congressman, one of the most important things about fishing is patience. In addition to that, sir, I do have a card with my address on it, and we have two fishing ponds at Troutlodge——

Mr. STENHOLM. Those work. I have always caught when I went into a pond. But stream fishing—and perhaps patience is the answer.

Mr. ZIMMERMAN. They are connected by a stream, sir, but we would love to have you.

Mr. STENHOLM. This subcommittee's jurisdiction—of course, Mr. Volkmer in livestock, is the subcommittee of jurisdiction from an agricultural perspective, but our jurisdiction stems from the organizational structure of USDA and how it fits as well as the research component.

And you talked about seeing that limited dollars will not be wasted on duplicative research. Do you have any examples today of where we perhaps are having already duplicative research? If not, just say so if you can't think of any. I can't. I am just curious.

I asked the question not so much as expecting an answer, but this subcommittee is the result of quite a bit of work that has gone on mostly behind the scenes with a research fellow that I had in my—not employ, but was there, and then having witnessed this year's round of Ag appropriations, have found that we really—the House Agriculture Committee really needs to spend some time and this subcommittee really needs to spend some time regarding the prioritization of research for all agriculture. With the scarce dollars that we have and the continued budget pressures that we will have, it is going to be imperative that we, in fact, begin serious looks and authorization of research priorities.

Aquaculture clearly is agriculture. There is no question about that. The sooner we establish that and have aquaculture receive its fair consideration within the scope of total agriculture, the better off certainly you are going to be, but I think the better off agriculture in general is going to be because we are no stronger than the weakest of our parts in agriculture.

The question again is timeliness, but certainly the 1995 farm bill is going to be the place in which you will sink or swim; no pun intended here. But you have a better chance, I think, of swimming, compared to some of the rest of the agricultural industry.

How is this bill different from the current legislative authority that we have; the Aquaculture Act of 1980? What is the major difference between current legislation and this? Anybody?

Mr. ZIMMERMAN. From a farmer's perspective, S. 1288 and H.R. 4744 provide clearer definitions. That is the area that we have focused on as clear differences.

Mr. MARTIN. You also had at that juncture three different Departments taking some role which never was clearly defined. This clearly defines it.

Mr. DOREY. Roles are clearly defined in this bill.

Mr. MCCRAREN. Definitions, research, the commercialization section, the education, language, credit, that is referenced, credit opportunities, disaster assistance and the like. It goes well beyond the act of 1980.

Mr. STENHOLM. Are you aware of any opposition to this legislation? If we were to report this, would there be someone coming forward and opposing it? Maybe some misguided youth?

No, seriously, are you aware of any opposition? It is rare that we have an industry come before the committee in which everybody in the industry is completely and totally united on legislation. That is a rarity.

Mr. McCRAREN. I see nothing but unity within this industry. If there is going to be a problem with the bill, I don't think there is anything new, different or exciting about this, but perhaps interagency considerations and the like. But beyond that, certainly not within this industry that I am aware of.

To a great degree, I should say, there may be some—some people, within the industry that might have a bit of a problem with some of it. But beyond that, at least with the people we represent and we deal with, they are certainly behind it.

Mr. STENHOLM. I am told that there is a difference between the Senate bill and this bill having to do with credit and commercialization, which were dropped from the Senate bill. Can you live with this bill if we do the same?

Mr. McCRAREN. We would prefer you didn't.

Mr. STENHOLM. Well, you will be thinking about that basic question, because if—and I am saying this is a gigantic if—as to whether we are going to be able to move legislation this week or not, but it is extremely important, if you are going to do that, that you have agreement. If there is a difference between the Senate language and the House language, then it makes it much less likely of getting a bill if there are significant differences.

I couldn't help but observe, I believe, Mr. McCraren, in your opening statement, you were giving the growth of the industry. The reason I was late to the hearing this morning, which I normally do not like to be, was because I was on the phone with a constituent that was rather irate and was—among many things, pointing out that agriculture is a subsidized industry and that we get cost-of-living adjustments every year but we have denied certain people cost-of-living adjustments and he was rather irate.

But in 1980, we were producing 203 million pounds of fish product in the United States; $192 million—94 cents a pound. In 1990, 860 million pounds valued at $760 million; a cost of 89 cents a pound. I can understand why in the bill you cite as one of your problems lack of adequate profit.

If these numbers are correct, and I assume that they are, the consumer is buying a wonderful product—and I am one of the best connoisseurs of catfish that you can find in Texas and we appreciate wherever it is produced. But here again, we have another example of the producing side actually in dollars producing it 5 cents a pound cheaper than was done in 1980.

Am I correct in my arithmetic?

Mr. McCRAREN. Based on those figures, yes.

Mr. MARTIN. As efficiencies of production develop, the cost literally comes down. The more that we have technology transfer and use that technology, the cost will come down even more.

Mr. DOREY. In 1980, we were raising some 3,000 pounds per acre of catfish per year. In 1990, we were up to 4,000 pounds per acre per year.

Mr. STENHOLM. That is another amazing success story for agriculture as an industry, one of which, quite frankly, the committee needs more of. We need more spokesmen telling the story. And, again, this subcommittee has the dual responsibility of technology and nutrition. And we are spending a lot of our time talking to nutritionists, and the so-called welfare community, those concerned about Americans who do not have, not only an adequate diet nutritionally in some cases but in volume in other cases.

And you know, it is a bad rap we get in production agriculture when we are accused of being the ones at fault and we have misguided witnesses that sit at this table from time to time and suggest that technology should be abolished—believe it or not, they sit there and say that—technology should be abolished because the things that we are using to produce more are somehow unhealthy. But this is a constant educational need that we have and one of which your industry certainly will be a very constructive partner in the overall agricultural story that we have to tell.

And I hope you can tell by that, I am very sympathetic to the bill, to the cause of what you are here to talk about. Certainly on the food safety standpoint, we have always believed that the Department of Agriculture's Food Safety and Inspection Service should be the predominant entity dealing with food safety.

You know of the conflict and the turf battles that we have been through and we will go through them again. But hopefully, with the reorganization bill that passed yesterday, we will have begun to set aside some of those problems with an entity within USDA now clearly authorized, and elevated to an Under Secretary level in which we will have someone with experience heading up that department, administration after administration, that we will begin to build the credibility within agriculture that will suffice in the public arena.

That is one of our many challenges.

Ms. Lambert, do have you any other questions of this panel?

Ms. LAMBERT. No, sir, but I would like to thank all of them from the organizational standpoint to the production side, and especially Mr. Dorey from my district, in realizing as he said the increase in production that we have realized from 1980 to 1990 is certainly proof that we can hang our hats on that, this is a serious industry and that it's been very productive in looking for resources to improve themselves.

We have the marketplace out there for them. Clearly if we have imports over 60 percent, we obviously have the marketplace here locally. But it almost staggers the imagination when you think what we could do to the trade deficit. We are the only surplus they have around here as you and I both know, and being big believers in agriculture, we would like to bring the aquaculture industry into the realm so that they could shed their positive light on again what agriculture can do for this Nation.

I would like to thank all the panelists and for their willingness to work with me. We look forward to being able to move this legislation if we—hopefully we can convince the Senate of the importance of all of the aspects of our bill here on the House side. And hopefully move something.

And thank you, Mr. Chairman, for your willingness to hold the hearing today.

Mr. STENHOLM. I want to ask about the numbers you gave me, now, that we have seen our production increase from 203 to 860, the cost per pound has declined, we are importing 9 billion dollars worth of fish products every year and we are producing 860 or—

less than 10 percent of what we consume we are producing domestically. We import the remainder.

I see the heads shaking.

Mr. PARKER. One clarification, Mr. Chairman. We also harvest from the natural fishery a significant amount of seafood. So the aquaculture production is only 10 percent of what we consume. But we also harvest from the seas quite a lot of shellfish from other sources.

Mr. STENHOLM. Identify yourself for the record.

Mr. PARKER. I am Hank Parker.

Mr. STENHOLM. Oh, I couldn't see back there, Dr. Parker.

One last question: Is there anything in this bill that would increase the regulatory burden on aquaculture producers; i.e., unfunded mandates, water quality assessment, anything that will possibly be defined as an unfunded mandate if we should pass this legislation?

Mr. MARTIN. I don't think so.

Mr. ZIMMERMAN. None that I know of.

Mr. STENHOLM. Scrutinize it with a fine tooth comb with us. That is a no-no.

Mr. Allard. You are recognized.

Mr. ALLARD. I had just a couple of questions that I am curious about.

Now, this legislation, I understand, treats aquatic plants and animals as livestock and agricultural commodities. Why is this important to your industry, if you would elaborate, please?

Mr. ZIMMERMAN. Sir, I am Jim Zimmerman representing Washington Fish Growers and my parent company Troutlodge, Incorporated. The most important aspect of having that definition is so that we can obtain services from the Animal and Plant Health Inspection Service of the USDA. We need to have our product certified as they move instate, intrastate and across international borders. At the moment, we don't have a consistent source for that certification.

APHIS could provide that consistent source and we have been working with them. Our university systems have been working with them in developing that. And what has been left open there is a clear definition of whether we are in or we are out, if you will. And fish need to be recognized as a livestock agricultural commodity so that these services can be provided.

Mr. ALLARD. Thank you for your response.

Another question I had is the legislation allows aquaculture to be eligible for disaster assistance. What sort of disasters does the industry face and can you give me an example of a situation when the industry needed access to disaster assistance?

Mr. MARTIN. I think one prime example was the floods along the Mississippi River that inundated some of the farms along the river that could have used assistance at that time. Flooding is one. A hurricane might be another.

Mr. DOREY. A few years back, we had an ice storm that the ponds froze over.

Mr. ALLARD. We have plants—aquatic plants get brought in as agricultural commodities. What examples of a crop would we have as an agricultural commodity that would be brought in?

Mr. ZIMMERMAN. Primarily seaweed.

Mr. ALLARD. I understand that to be a food. Now, is that grown with freshwater or saltwater?

Mr. MARTIN. It can be grown with both. The saltwater variety yields us a product called carrageenan which then goes into a host of food products as a thickener and an emulsifier.

Mr. ALLARD. Now, we are in the process of trying to cover our commodities with a crop insurance plan, Mr. Chairman, and I am wondering how everybody is visualizing this might work, and someday there might be crop insurance that would be available for somebody who has plants that would fall under the definition of aquaculture?

Is the industry visualizing this kind of a program or are you visualizing that there may be a flood that would wipe out a seaweed farm and that you would come into this Congress for an emergency appropriation?

Mr. MCCRAREN. I would just say, sir, that in a sense, the aquatic plants are embraced as a part of the definition of aquaculture that, in our minds, they would be included certainly.

Mr. ALLARD. You want them included as part of the crop insurance program or are you thinking in terms of staying out of the program and then coming in and asking for emergency assistance when disaster occurs?

Mr. MCCRAREN. Well, right now, the two bills referenced relief in terms of disaster assistance. I have heard, however, that there is the possibility of someone offering crop insurance as an alternative but we haven't examined that personally ourselves.

Mr. ALLARD. Is that your preferred way to go?

Mr. MCCRAREN. I couldn't answer on behalf of my group. We haven't examined it. We are supportive, however, of the industry being considered for disaster assistance, per se.

Mr. ALLARD. I think we need to sit back and kind of—look kind of seriously at some of these things and not see what our policy ought to be and not wait until a disaster occurs and try to deal with it. And I think your industry has to let us know in which direction you want to go as far as crop insurance or not, and how you want to go about maybe managing the disasters, taking some personal responsibility for those we manage—these disasters from your own industry.

Mr. MCCRAREN. One point was that we didn't want to be treated any better than anyone else, but certainly we didn't want to be treated any differently with regard to being a member of the agricultural community, with regard to disaster assistance.

Mr. ALLARD. Thank you.

Mr. STENHOLM. Are you able to buy insurance today for protection against the kind of catastrophes that you are talking about?

Mr. DOREY. Not a catfish farmer.

Mr. STENHOLM. None available? You can insure cows, sheep, and pigs.

Mr. DOREY. Maybe Lloyds of London. I don't know. But other than that, that is——

Mr. STENHOLM. That is a good point Mr. Allard was raising, because—and you are going to need to give some thought to this as a result of how you establish eligibility for even disaster relief because, as you read this morning's paper, as we find we have some terrific problems with nontraditional payment of disaster.

And by nontraditional, I mean where you have a record of production and you have some history to go by regarding what is a loss and how much and how you count it and how you weigh it. It is a terrific problem and one which we are going to have to give a lot of thought to as we proceed along that line, working with the administration.

Thank you all very much for being here. I would ask—I see, Dr. Parker, you are still here. If your time would permit, I would appreciate you meeting with the staff and Mr. Volkmer or myself and Chairman de la Garza and sitting down and seeing how we might be able to proceed, if at all.

And we thank all the witnesses for being here this morning.

Ms. Lambert, thank you very much for your work in bringing and seeing that this legislation gets to this point.

Thank you all very much. The subcommittees are adjourned.

[Whereupon, at 11:25 a.m., the joint subcommittees were adjourned, to reconvene subject to the call of the respective Chairs.]

[Material submitted for inclusion in the record follows:]

I

103D CONGRESS
2D SESSION

H. R. 4744

To provide for the coordination and implementation of a national aquaculture policy for the private sector by the Secretary of Agriculture, to establish an aquaculture commercialization research program, and for other purposes.

IN THE HOUSE OF REPRESENTATIVES

JULY 13, 1994

Ms. LAMBERT (for herself, Mr. THORNTON, Mr. EMERSON, Mr. STENHOLM, Mr. MCCLOSKEY, Mr. HILLIARD, and Mr. BAKER of Louisiana) introduced the following bill; which was referred to the Committee on Agriculture

---

A BILL

To provide for the coordination and implementation of a national aquaculture policy for the private sector by the Secretary of Agriculture, to establish an aquaculture commercialization research program, and for other purposes.

Be it enacted by the Senate and House of Representatives of the United States of America in Congress assembled,

SECTION 1. SHORT TITLE AND TABLE OF CONTENTS.

(a) SHORT TITLE.—This Act may be cited as the "National Aquaculture Development, Commercialization, and Promotion Act of 1994".

(b) TABLE OF CONTENTS.—The table of contents of this Act is as follows:

SEC. 2. FINDINGS AND PURPOSE.

(a) FINDINGS.—Subsection (a) of section 2 of the National Aquaculture Act of 1980 (16 U.S.C. 2801) is amended to read as follows:

"(a) FINDINGS.—Congress finds the following:

"(1) The wild harvest or capture of certain seafood species exceeds levels of optimum sustainable yield, thereby making it more difficult to meet the increasing demand for aquatic food.

"(2) To satisfy the domestic market for aquatic food, the United States imports more than 59 percent of its seafood. This dependence on imports adversely affects the national balance of payments and

87-941 O - 95 - 3

contributes to the uncertainty of supplies and product quality.

"(3) Although aquaculture currently contributes approximately 16 percent by weight of world seafood production, less than 9 percent by weight of current United States seafood production results from aquaculture. As a result, domestic aquaculture production has the potential for significant growth.

"(4) Aquaculture production of aquatic animals and plants is a source of food, industrial materials, pharmaceuticals, energy, and aesthetic enjoyment, and can assist in the control and abatement of pollution.

"(5) The rehabilitation and enhancement of fish and shellfish resources are desirable applications of aquaculture technology.

"(6) The principal responsibility for the development of aquaculture in the United States must rest with the private sector.

"(7) Despite its potential, the development of aquaculture in the United States has been inhibited by many scientific, economic, legal, and production factors, such as—

"(A) inadequate credit;

"(B) limited research and development and demonstration programs;

"(C) diffused legal jurisdiction;

"(D) inconsistent interpretations between Federal agencies;

"(E) the lack of management information;

"(F) the lack of supportive policies of the Federal Government;

"(G) the lack of therapeutic compounds for treatment of the diseases of aquatic animals and plants; and

"(H) the lack of reliable supplies of seed stock.

"(8) Many areas of the United States are suitable for aquaculture, but are subject to land-use or water-use management policies and regulations that do not adequately consider the potential for aquaculture and may inhibit the development of aquaculture.

"(9) In 1990, the United States ranked only tenth in the world in aquaculture production based on total value of products.

"(10) Despite the current and increasing importance of private aquaculture to the United States economy and to rural areas in the United States,

Federal efforts to nurture aquaculture development have failed to keep pace with the needs of fish and aquatic plant farmers.

"(11) The United States has a premier opportunity to expand existing aquaculture production and develop new aquaculture industries to serve national needs and the global marketplace.

"(12) United States aquaculture provides wholesome products for domestic consumers and contributes significantly to employment opportunities and the quality of life in rural areas in the United States.

"(13) Since 1980, the United States trade deficit in edible fishery products has increased by 48 percent, from $1,777,921,000 to $2,634,738,000 in 1991.

"(14) Aquaculture is poised to become a major growth industry of the 21st century. With global seafood demand projected to increase 70 percent by 2025, and harvests from capture fisheries stable or declining, aquaculture would have to increase production by 700 percent, a total of 77 million metric tons annually.

"(15) Private aquaculture production in the United States has increased an average of 20 percent by weight annually since 1980, and is one of the fastest growing segments of United States and world agriculture.

"(16) In 1990, private United States aquaculture production was 860,750,000 pounds, worth $761,500,000, up from 203,178,000 pounds, worth $191,977,000, in 1980.

"(17) Since 1960, per capita consumption of aquatic foods in the United States has increased by 49 percent to 14.9 pounds in 1991, and could reach 20 pounds by the year 2000. Total United States demand is projected to double by 2020.".

(b) PURPOSE.—Subsection (b) of such section (16 U.S.C. 2801) is amended to read as follows:

"(b) PURPOSE.—It is the purpose of this Act to promote aquaculture in the United States by—

"(1) declaring a national aquaculture policy;

"(2) establishing private aquaculture as a form of agriculture;

"(3) establishing cultivated aquatic animals, plants, microorganisms, and their products produced by private persons and moving in standard commodity channels as agricultural livestock, crops, and commodities;

"(4) establishing the Department as the lead Federal agency for the development, implementation, promotion, and coordination of national policy and programs for private aquaculture by—

"(A) designating the Secretary as the permanent chairperson of a Federal interagency aquaculture coordinating group;

"(B) assigning overall responsibility to the Secretary for coordinating, developing, and carrying out policies and programs for private aquaculture; and

"(C) authorizing the establishment of a National Aquaculture Information Center within the Department to support the United States aquaculture industry; and

"(5) encouraging—

"(A) aquaculture activities and programs in both the public and private sectors of the economy of the United States;

"(B) the creation of new industries and job opportunities related to aquaculture activities;

"(C) the reduction of the fisheries trade deficit; and

"(D) other national policy benefits deriving from aquaculture activities.".

SEC. 3. DEFINITIONS.

Section 3 of the National Aquaculture Act of 1980 (16 U.S.C. 2802) is amended—

(1) in the matter before the paragraphs, by striking "requires—" and inserting "requires:";

(2) by striking paragraph (1) and inserting the following new paragraph:

"(1) The term 'aquaculture' means the controlled cultivation of aquatic plants, animals, and microorganisms. Such term does not include private cultivation of Pacific salmon for profit in those States where such cultivation is prohibited by law.";

(3) in paragraph (3), by inserting before the period at the end the following: "or microorganism";

(4) by redesignating paragraphs (7) through (9) as paragraphs (9) through (11), respectively;

(5) by redesignating paragraphs (5) and (6) as paragraphs (6) and (7), respectively;

(6) by inserting after paragraph (4) the following new paragraph:

"(5) The term 'Department' means the United States Department of Agriculture."; and

(7) by inserting before paragraph (9) (as redesignated by paragraph (4)) the following new paragraph:

"(8) The term 'private aquaculture' means the controlled cultivation of aquatic plants, animals, and microorganisms other than cultivation carried out by the Federal Government or any State or local government.".

SEC. 4. NATIONAL AQUACULTURE DEVELOPMENT PLAN.

Section 4 of the National Aquaculture Act of 1980 (16 U.S.C. 2803) is amended—

(1) in the second sentence of subsection (c)—

(A) in subparagraph (A), by adding "and" at the end;

(B) in subparagraph (B), by striking "; and" and inserting a period; and

(C) by striking subparagraph (C);

(2) in the second sentence of subsection (d), by striking "Secretaries determine" and inserting "Secretary, in consultation with the other Secretaries, determines";

(3) in subsection (e)—

(A) by striking "Secretaries" and inserting "Secretary"; and

(B) by inserting "and in consultation with the other Secretaries and representatives of other Federal agencies" after "coordinating group"; and

(4) by adding at the end the following new subsection:

"(f) ACCOMPLISHMENTS IN AQUACULTURE PROGRAMS.—Not later than December 31, 1994, the Secretary, in consultation with the Secretary of Commerce and the Secretary of the Interior, shall submit to Congress a report evaluating the actions taken in accordance with subsection (d) with respect to the Plan, and making recommendations for updating and modifying the Plan. The report shall also contain a compendium on Federal regulations relating to aquaculture.".

SEC. 5. NATIONAL AQUACULTURE INFORMATION CENTER AND ASSIGNMENT OF NEW PROGRAMS.

Section 5 of the National Aquaculture Act of 1980 (16 U.S.C. 2804) is amended—

(1) in subsection (b)(3), by striking "Secretaries deem" and inserting "Secretary, in consultation with the other Secretaries, considers";

(2) in subsection (c)(1)(B)—

(A) by striking clause (i) and inserting the following new clause:

"(i) establish, within the Department, within the National Agricultural Library, a National Aquaculture Information Center that shall—

"(I) serve as a repository and clearinghouse for the information collected under subparagraph (A) and other provisions of this Act;

"(II) carry out a program to notify organizations, institutions, and individuals known to be involved in aquaculture of the existence of the Center and the kinds of information that the Center can make available to the public; and

"(III) make available, on request, information described in subclause (I) (including information collected under subsection (e));"; and

(B) in clause (ii), by striking the comma and inserting a semicolon;

(3) in the first sentence of subsection (d), by striking "Interior,," and inserting "Interior,"; and

(4) by adding at the end the following new subsection:

"(e) ASSIGNMENT OF NEW PROGRAMS.—In consultation with representatives of the United States aquaculture industry and in coordination with the Secretary of the Interior, the Secretary of Commerce, and the heads of other appropriate Federal agencies, the Secretary shall assess

Federal aquatic animal health programs and make recommendations as to the appropriate assignment to Federal agencies of new programs, initiatives, and activities in support of aquaculture and resource stewardship and management.".

SEC. 6. COORDINATION WITH THE AQUACULTURE INDUSTRY.

Section 6(b) of the National Aquaculture Act of 1980 (16 U.S.C. 2805(b)) is amended—

(1) in paragraph (5), by striking "and" at the end;

(2) in paragraph (6), by striking the period at the end and inserting "; and"; and

(3) by adding at the end the following new paragraph:

"(7) in order to facilitate improved communication and interaction among aquaculture producers, the aquaculture community, the Federal Government, and the coordinating group, establish a working relationship with—

"(A) the industry advisory councils of the regional aquaculture centers established by the Secretary under section 1475(d) of the National Agricultural Research, Extension, and Teaching Policy Act of 1977 (7 U.S.C. 3322(d)); and

"(B) national organizations, commodity associations, and professional societies representing aquaculture interests.".

SEC. 7. AQUACULTURE COMMERCIALIZATION PROGRAM.

The National Aquaculture Act of 1980 (16 U.S.C. 2801 et seq.) is amended—

(1) by redesignating sections 7 through 11 as sections 14 through 18, respectively; and

(2) by inserting after section 6 the following new section:

"SEC. 7. AQUACULTURE COMMERCIALIZATION PROGRAM.

"(a) DEFINITIONS.—As used in this section, the term 'eligible entity' means a private company, public or private research or educational organization, regional center, Federal, State, or regional agency, or individual that is eligible to receive a grant or enter into a contract under this section.

"(b) ASSISTANCE AND COORDINATION.—

"(1) IN GENERAL.—The Secretary may make grants and enter into contracts with eligible entities to pay the Federal share of projects to support the market development and commercialization of aquaculture research findings and technologies that—

"(A) demonstrate strong potential for accelerating the transfer to the marketplace of aquaculture products, processes, and technologies that can improve profitability, production efficiency, and sustainability of existing and emerging aquaculture sectors;

"(B) will help the United States aquaculture industry to be more competitive in the global marketplace; and

"(C) will facilitate the commercialization of promising research and technologies deriving from existing research programs.

"(2) COST SHARE.—

"(A) FEDERAL SHARE.—Except as provided in subparagraph (B), the Federal share of the cost of a project carried out under this program shall be 80 percent.

"(B) REMAINING SHARE.—The remaining share of the cost of a project carried out under this program may be—

"(i) in the form of cash or in-kind payments, or both; and

"(ii) partially comprised of funds made available under other Federal programs, except that the non-Federal share of the project may not be less than 10 percent of the cost of the project.

"(c) PRIORITIES.—In making grants or entering into contracts under subsection (b), the Secretary shall give priority to—

"(1) field testing, commercial field trials, market development programs, and applications of aquaculture research to private aquaculture that would promote the transfer of promising aquaculture technologies to the market place; and

"(2) projects carried out under commercial conditions at private, commercial aquaculture facilities.

"(d) COMPETITIVE REVIEW.—

"(1) IN GENERAL.—To be eligible to receive a grant or enter into a contract under subsection (b), a proposal shall undergo competitive review.

"(2) COMPETITIVE REVIEW PANELS.—A competitive review panel shall be composed of individuals appointed by the Secretary who understand the aquaculture industry and sound business practices and are qualified to objectively evaluate the likelihood of a proposal being economically successful or promoting economic success within the aquaculture industry. Review panels shall equitably represent the United States aquaculture community and shall be developed in close consultation with aquaculture industry leaders.

"(3) EVALUATION.—A competitive review panel shall base an evaluation of a proposal under this subsection on—

"(A) the quality of the proposal and the proposed methodology;

"(B) the capability of the participating entity to perform the proposed work;

"(C) the potential for fostering commercialization, job creation, and increased sales of aquaculture products;

"(D) the amount of matching funds provided by the supported entity or obtained from non-Federal sources;

"(E) the extent of collaboration with other Federal and State programs;

"(F) the existence of a sound business plan that reasonably projects the benefits of the support being requested;

"(G) in the case of a noncommercial entity, the existence of a cooperative agreement with a commercial entity;

"(H) whether the project would promote responsible environmental stewardship; and

"(I) such other factors as the competitive review panel determines to be appropriate.

"(e) LIMITATIONS.—

"(1) ADMINISTRATIVE EXPENSES.—Not more than 3 percent of the amounts made available to carry out this section during a fiscal year may be used by the Secretary for the expenses of administration and information collection and dissemination.

"(2) CONSTRUCTION COSTS.—None of the funds made available under this section may be used for the construction of a new building or the acquisition, expansion, remodeling, or alteration of an existing building (including site grading and improvement and architect fees).

"(f) REPORTS.—An eligible entity that receives a grant or enters into a contract under a project carried out under this section shall submit an annual progress report, and a final report, to the Secretary that—

"(1) describes project activities and commercial and economic accomplishments and impacts; and

"(2) in the case of an annual progress report, includes a project plan for the subsequent year.

"(g) AUTHORIZATION OF APPROPRIATIONS.—There are authorized to be appropriated such sums as are necessary to carry out this section.".

SEC. 8. NATIONAL POLICY FOR PRIVATE AQUACULTURE.

The National Aquaculture Act of 1980 (16 U.S.C. 2801 et seq.) is amended by inserting after section 7 (as added by section 7(2)) the following new section:

"SEC. 8. NATIONAL POLICY FOR PRIVATE AQUACULTURE.

"(a) IN GENERAL.—The Secretary, in consultation with the Secretary of Commerce, the Secretary of the Interior, and the heads of other agencies, as appropriate, shall coordinate and implement a national policy for private aquaculture in accordance with this section.

"(b) DEPARTMENT AQUACULTURE PLAN.—

"(1) IN GENERAL.—The Secretary shall develop and implement a Department Aquaculture Plan (referred to in this section as the 'plan') for a unified Department aquaculture program to support the development of private United States aquaculture.

"(2) ELEMENTS OF PLAN.—The plan shall address—

"(A) individual agency programs related to aquaculture in the Department that are consistent with Department programs applied to other agricultural programs, livestock, crops, products, and commodities under the jurisdiction of Department agencies;

"(B) the treatment of cultivated aquatic animals as livestock and cultivated aquatic plants as agricultural crops; and

"(C) means for effective coordination and implementation of aquaculture activities and programs within the Department, including individual agency commitments of personnel and resources.

"(3) DEADLINE.—Not later than 1 year after the date of enactment of the National Aquaculture Development, Research, and Promotion Act of 1994, the Secretary shall submit the plan to Congress.

"(4) REPORTS.—Not later than 1 year after the date of the submission of the plan pursuant to paragraph (3), and annually thereafter, the Secretary shall report to Congress on actions taken to implement the plan during the year preceding the date of the report.

"(5) NATIONAL AQUACULTURE INFORMATION CENTER.—

"(A) IN GENERAL.—In carrying out section 5, the Secretary may maintain and support a National Aquaculture Information Center (referred to in this paragraph as the 'Center') as a repository for information on national and international aquaculture.

"(B) PUBLIC ACCESS.—Information in the Center shall be made available to the public.

"(C) INTERNATIONAL EXCHANGE.—The head of the Center shall arrange with foreign nations for the exchange of information relating to aquaculture and shall support a translation service.

"(D) SUPPORT.—The Center shall provide direct support to the coordinating group.

"(c) NATIONAL AQUACULTURE DEVELOPMENT PLAN.—

"(1) IN GENERAL.—Not later than 1 year after the date of enactment of the National Aquaculture Development, Research, and Promotion Act of 1994, the Secretary shall revise the National Aquaculture Development Plan required to be established under section 4.

"(2) COORDINATION.—The Secretary shall integrate and coordinate the aquaculture and related missions, major objectives, and program components of individual aquaculture plans of the coordinating group members.

"(3) SUBMISSION TO CONGRESS.—Not later than 1 year after the date of enactment of the National Aquaculture Development, Research, and Promotion Act of 1994, the Secretary shall submit a revised Plan to Congress.

"(4) UPDATES.—Not later than 5 years after the date of the submission of the revised Plan pursuant to paragraph (3), and annually thereafter, the Secretary shall revise the National Aquaculture Development Plan.

"(d) TREATMENT OF AQUACULTURE.—The Secretary shall, for all purposes, treat—

"(1) private aquaculture as a form of agriculture; and

"(2) cultivated aquatic animals, plants, and microorganisms, and products of the animals, plants, and microorganisms, produced by private persons and moving in standard commodity channels as agricultural livestock, crops, and commodities.

"(e) RESOLUTION OF INTERAGENCY CONFLICT.—In consultation with representatives of affected Federal agencies, the Secretary shall be responsible for resolving any interagency conflict in the coordination or implementation of the policy described in this section.

"(f) PRIVATE AQUACULTURE POLICY COORDINATION, DEVELOPMENT, AND IMPLEMENTATION.—

"(1) RESPONSIBILITY.—The Secretary shall have overall responsibility for coordinating, developing, and carrying out policies and programs for private aquaculture.

"(2) DUTIES.—The Secretary shall—

"(A) coordinate all intradepartmental functions and activities relating to private aquaculture;

"(B) establish procedures for the coordination of functions, and consultation, with the coordinating group; and

"(C) recommend to the National Agricultural Library methods by which the aquaculture resources of the Library can be made more easily retrievable and can be more widely disseminated.

"(3) LIAISON.—

"(A) AGENCIES OF THE DEPARTMENT.—To facilitate communication and interaction between the aquaculture community and the Department, the head of each agency of the Department shall, if requested by the Secretary, designate an officer or employee of the agency to be the liaison of the agency with the Secretary.

"(B) DEPARTMENTS OF COMMERCE AND THE INTERIOR.—The Secretary of Commerce and the Secretary of the Interior shall each designate an officer or employee of their respective Departments to be the liaison of their respective Departments with the Secretary.".

SEC. 9. WATER QUALITY ASSESSMENT.

The National Aquaculture Act of 1980 (16 U.S.C. 2801 et seq.) is amended by inserting after section 8 (as added by section 8) the following new section:

"SEC. 9. WATER QUALITY ASSESSMENT.

"(a) ASSESSMENT.—The Administrator of the Environmental Protection Agency is authorized to carry out, in collaboration with the Secretary, collaborative interagency programs that demonstrate the application of aquaculture to environmental enhancement and assessment, including a program to assess the environmental impact of waterborne contaminants on naturally occurring aquatic organisms and ecosystems using aquaculture-raised organisms to serve as an indicator of environmental pollution.

"(b) GRANTS; COOPERATIVE AGREEMENTS.—The Administrator may provide grants or enter into cooperative agreements or contracts with private research organizations for research and demonstration of the technology authorized by this section.".

SEC. 10. NATIVE AMERICAN FISHPOND REVITALIZATION.

The National Aquaculture Act of 1980 (16 U.S.C. 2801 et seq.) is amended by inserting after section 9 (as added by section 9) the following new section:

"SEC. 10. NATIVE AMERICAN FISHPOND REVITALIZATION.

"(a) DEFINITION OF NATIVE AMERICAN.—As used in this section, the term 'Native American' means—

"(1) an Indian, as defined in section 4(d) of the Indian Self-Determination and Education Assistance Act (25 U.S.C. 450b(d));

"(2) a Native Hawaiian, as defined in section 8(3) of the Native Hawaiian Health Care Act of 1988 (42 U.S.C. 11707(3)) or section 815(3) of the Native American Programs Act (42 U.S.C. 2992c(3));

"(3) an Alaska Native, within the meaning provided for the term 'Native' in section 3(b) of the Alaska Native Claims Settlement Act (43 U.S.C. 1602(b)); and

"(4) a Pacific Islander, within the meaning of the Native American Programs Act of 1974 (42 U.S.C. 2991 et seq.).

"(b) AUTHORIZATION OF PROGRAM.—The Secretary of Agriculture is authorized to carry out a program to revitalize fishponds used by Native Americans to cultivate aquatic species.

"(c) GRANTS; COOPERATIVE AGREEMENTS.—The Secretary may provide grants or enter into cooperative agreements with individuals and organizations, including Native American organizations, to promote fishpond revitalization. Funds provided under this section may be used to engage in fishpond research, pond culture technology development, the application of traditional pond culture techniques and modern aquaculture practices to ancient fishponds, technical assistance and technology transfer, and such other activities as the Secretary determines are appropriate.".

SEC. 11. DISASTER ASSISTANCE FOR AQUACULTURE FARMS.

(a) IN GENERAL.—Section 2244 of the Food, Agriculture, Conservation, and Trade Act of 1990 (7 U.S.C. 1421 note) is amended—

(1) in subsection (a)(1)(A)(ii), by inserting ", if applicable," after "subsection (d)(2) for such crop"; and

(2) in subsection (d)(1), by inserting "and cultivated aquatic species," after "was not available for crop year 1990,".

(b) LIMITATION.—The amendments made by subsection (a) shall apply only to the extent appropriations are made available after the date of enactment of this Act to carry out the amendments.

(c) ELIGIBILITY.—Notwithstanding any other provision of law, aquaculture producers shall be eligible for disaster assistance for 1993 crop losses under the same terms and conditions as are specified in chapter 3 of subtitle B of title XXII of the Food, Agriculture, Conservation, and Trade Act of 1990 (7 U.S.C. 1421 note).

SEC. 12. AQUACULTURE EDUCATION.

The National Aquaculture Act of 1980 (16 U.S.C. 2801 et seq.) is amended by inserting after section 10 (as added by section 10) the following new section:

"SEC. 11. AQUACULTURE EDUCATION.

"(a) DEFINITIONS.—As used in this section:

"(1) POSTSECONDARY VOCATIONAL INSTITUTION.—The term 'postsecondary vocational institution' has the same meaning given the term by section 481(c) of the Higher Education Act of 1965 (20 U.S.C. 1088(c)), except that the term only includes an institution that awards an associates degree but does not award a bachelor's degree.

"(2) SECONDARY SCHOOL.—The term 'secondary school' has the same meaning given the term by section 1471(21) of the Elementary and Secondary Education Act of 1965 (20 U.S.C. 2891(21)).

"(b) AUTHORIZATION OF PROGRAM.—The Secretary is authorized to establish a program to expand and improve instruction, on aquaculture and the basic principles of aquaculture farming, in the agriculture curriculum for students attending secondary schools and postsecondary vocational institutions.

"(c) GRANTS AND CURRICULUM.—In carrying out subsection (b), the Secretary may—

"(1) make grants to—

"(A) establish and maintain aquaculture learning centers in secondary schools and postsecondary vocational institutions;

"(B) promote aquaculture technology transfer; and

"(C) educate consumers and the public concerning the benefits of aquaculture; and

"(2) develop curriculum and supporting materials on aquaculture farming, field test the content of the curriculum, and supply training to educators at secondary schools and postsecondary vocational institutions on the aquaculture curriculum and materials developed.

"(d) PRIORITY FOR GRANTS.—In awarding grants under subsection (c)(1), the Secretary shall give priority to—

"(1) the ability of the proposed aquaculture learning center to gain access to—

"(A) a commercial aquaculture farm;

"(B) a regional aquaculture center established by the Secretary under section 1475(d) of the National Agricultural Research, Extension, and Teaching Policy Act of 1977 (7 U.S.C. 3322(d));

"(C) an aquaculture research facility; or

"(D) a similar venture that would afford students the opportunity to experience aquaculture research and development or commercialization;

"(2) the ability of the center to achieve outreach to minority audiences or students in inner-city schools;

"(3) the ability of the center to foster awareness of aquaculture among consumers and the general public;

"(4) the ability of the center to serve as an aquaculture education facility for visiting students participating in a field trip or a similar educational experience for inservice training; and

"(5) the level of assistance to be provided from non-Federal sources.

"(e) LIMITATION.—

"(1) IN GENERAL.—Except as provided in paragraph (2), a grantee may not receive a grant under this section for more than 5 fiscal years.

"(2) WAIVER.—In the case of grantees that receive grants under this section for fiscal year 1995, the Secretary may waive the application of paragraph (1) to the grantees for the fiscal year if the Secretary determines that the application of paragraph (1) to the grantees would result in the termination of an excessive number of grants.".

SEC. 13. INTERNATIONAL AQUACULTURE SCIENTIFIC EXCHANGE.

The National Aquaculture Act of 1980 (16 U.S.C. 2801 et seq.) is amended by inserting after section 11 (as added by section 12) the following new section:

"SEC. 12. INTERNATIONAL AQUACULTURE SCIENTIFIC EXCHANGE.

"(a) DEFINITION OF ELIGIBLE ENTITY.—As used in this section, the term 'eligible entity' means a regional aquaculture center, college, university, or nonprofit organization engaged in aquaculture research and education in the United States or a foreign country.

"(b) GRANTS.—The Secretary may make grants to eligible entities to defray the cost, in whole or in part, of allowing aquaculture researchers and aquaculture technologists to engage in research, education, and demonstration at the eligible entities for periods of up to 2 years.

"(c) FUNDING.—The Secretary may use proceeds from the payments referred to in section 104(a) of the Agricultural Trade Development and Assistance Act of 1954 (7 U.S.C. 1704(a)) to carry out this section.".

SEC. 14. AUTHORIZATION OF APPROPRIATIONS.

The first sentence of section 17 of the National Aquaculture Act of 1980 (as redesignated by section 7(1)) is amended to read as follows: "There are authorized to be appropriated to carry out this Act to the Department $2,000,000 for each of fiscal years 1995 and 1996 (of which not less than $500,000 shall be used for each fiscal year to carry out the Joint Subcommittee on Aquaculture established under section 6(a)), to the Department of Commerce $500,000 for each of fiscal years 1995 and

1996, and to the Department of the Interior $500,000 for each of fiscal years 1995 and 1996.".

SEC. 15. ELIGIBILITY OF AQUACULTURE FARMERS FOR FARM CREDIT ASSISTANCE.

(a) IN GENERAL.—Section 343 of the Consolidated Farm and Rural Development Act (7 U.S.C. 1991) is amended by striking "fish farming" both places it appears in paragraphs (1) and (2) and inserting "aquaculture (as the term is defined in section 3(1) of the National Aquaculture Act of 1980 (16 U.S.C. 2802(1)))".

(b) EFFECTIVE DATE.—The amendments made by subsection (a) shall become effective on October 1, 1994.

SEC. 16. INTERNATIONAL AQUACULTURE INFORMATION AND DATA COLLECTION.

Section 502 of the Agricultural Trade Act of 1978 (7 U.S.C. 5692) is amended by adding at the end the following new subsection:

"(d) INTERNATIONAL AQUACULTURE INFORMATION AND DATA COLLECTION.—

"(1) IN GENERAL.—The Secretary is authorized to establish and carry out a program of data collection, analysis, and dissemination of information to provide continuing and timely economic information concerning international aquaculture production.

"(2) CONSULTATION.—In carrying out paragraph (1), the Secretary shall consult with the Joint Subcommittee on Aquaculture established under section 6(a) of the National Aquaculture Act of 1980 (16 U.S.C. 2805(a)), and representatives of the United States aquaculture industry, concerning means of effectively providing data described in paragraph (1) to the Joint Subcommittee and the industry.".

SEC. 17. ELIGIBILITY OF AQUACULTURE FARMS FOR EMERGENCY CONSERVATION PROGRAM.

Section 401 of the Agricultural Credit Act of 1978 (16 U.S.C. 2201) is amended—

(1) by inserting "or aquaculture farms" after "farmlands" both places it appears; and

(2) by inserting "or aquaculture farm" after "land" each place it appears.

SEC. 18. AQUACULTURE INFORMATION NETWORK REPORT.

Not later than 180 days after the date of enactment of this Act, the Secretary of Agriculture shall report to Congress on the feasibility of expanding current information systems at regional aquaculture centers established by the Secretary under section 1475(d) of the National Agricultural Research, Extension, and Teaching Policy Act of 1977 (7 U.S.C. 3322(d)), universities, research institutions, and the National Agricultural Library to permit an on-line link between those entities for the sharing of data, publication, and technical assistance information involving aquaculture.

SEC. 19. VOLUNTARY CERTIFICATION OF QUALITY STANDARDS.

The National Aquaculture Act of 1980 (16 U.S.C. 2801 et seq.) is amended by inserting after section 12 (as added by section 13) the following new section:

"SEC. 13. VOLUNTARY CERTIFICATION OF QUALITY STANDARDS.

"The Secretary shall develop, in consultation with representatives of the aquaculture industry, a plan for voluntary certification of guidelines to ensure the quality of aquatic species subject to this Act in order to promote the marketing and transportation of aquaculture products.".

SEC. 20. IMPLEMENTATION REPORT.

(a) IN GENERAL.—Not later than 180 days after the date of enactment of this Act, the Secretary of Agriculture shall report to Congress on the progress made in carrying out this Act and the amendments made by this Act.

(b) CONTENTS.—The report required by subsection (a) shall include—

(1) a description of all programs and activities of the Department of Agriculture and all other agen-

cies and Departments in support of private aquaculture;

(2) the specific authorities for the activities described in paragraph (1); and

(3) recommendations for such actions as the Secretary of Agriculture determines are necessary to improve recognition and support of private aquaculture in each agency of the Department of Agriculture.

○

STATEMENT OF
HENRY S. PARKER
U.S. DEPARTMENT OF AGRICULTURE
BEFORE THE
SUBCOMMITTEE ON DEPARTMENT OPERATIONS AND NUTRITION
OF THE
COMMITTEE ON AGRICULTURE
UNITED STATES HOUSE OF REPRESENTATIVES
OCTOBER 4, 1994

Mr. Chairman and Members of the Subcommittee, I appreciate the opportunity to present testimony on behalf of the Department of Agriculture on H.R. 4744, "The National Aquaculture Development, Commercialization, and Promotion Act of 1994."

Aquaculture will be a major, global agricultural growth industry in the 21st century. The United States has an important opportunity to develop an internationally competitive aquaculture industry to serve national needs and the global marketplace. Currently, the United States ranks only tenth in the world in the value of its aquaculture industry, and imports over 60 percent of its seafood from other countries.

Mr. Chairman, I would like to comment briefly on the bill. Because of the limited time available, we have not been able to consult fully with other affected agencies. Consequently, these comments do not reflect the Administration's position. However, I can say that the Administration looks forward to working closely with the bill's sponsors on similar legislation during the 104th Congress.

H.R. 4744 would amend and reauthorize the National Aquaculture Act of 1980. The bill would strengthen and broaden USDA's leadership role in support of private aquaculture by designating USDA as "the lead Federal agency for the development, implementation, promotion, and coordination of national policy and programs for private aquaculture...".

The Department recognizes that H.R. 4744 is a bill for private, commercial aquaculture. The Secretary of Agriculture is committed to strong Departmental leadership of collaborative, interagency programs to support the private U.S. aquaculture industry. The Department recognizes that aquaculture is an important, growing segment of U.S. agriculture that has great potential for jobs creation, rural economies, reduction of the trade deficit, and supplying nutritious, healthful food for U.S. consumers.

The bill would enable the Secretary of Agriculture to provide a stronger Federal leadership role through the Joint Subcommittee on Aquaculture (JSA) which has become an effective and influential interagency coordinating body. The Secretary welcomes the opportunity to continue to provide strong leadership to this body.

The Department also recognizes that other agencies have programs and interests that can support both private and public aquaculture. However, effective leadership by the Department of Agriculture can promote the continued development of a healthy aquatic farming industry by facilitating cooperation among these agencies. In line with this, the Department recommends modifying Section 5 of H.R. 4744 to delete proposed new Section 5 (e) of the National Aquaculture Act of 1980 ("Assignment of New Programs"). This section would authorize the Secretary to assess Federal aquatic animal health programs and to make recommendations as to the appropriate assignment to Federal agencies of new programs. In making such recommendations, Section 5 (e) would require the Secretary to consult with representatives of the U.S. aquaculture industry and coordinate with the Secretaries of the Interior and Commerce and the heads of other appropriate Federal agencies. Such a review of agency programs, however, is more appropriately done on a collaborative basis by the agencies involved. The Department is already working with other members of the Joint Subcommittee on Aquaculture (JSA) to review all issues on aquatic animal health.

The bill would promote private aquaculture by "establishing private aquaculture as a form of agriculture and establishing cultivated aquatic animals, plants, microorganisms, and their products, produced by private persons and moving in standard commodity channels as agricultural livestock, crops, and commodities." The Department recognizes that private, commercial aquaculture is an important and growing form of agriculture. The Department is committed to providing a broad range of services for this industry. For example, the Department wishes to work closely with the industry to provide a full range of health services for cultivated aquatic animals. In order to provide aquatic animal health programs, as are currently provided for other production animals, the Animal and Plant Health Inspection Service will continue to work closely with other members of the JSA to develop legislative recommendations to address this issue.

The Department notes that H.R. 4744 would retain Section 11 of the National Aquaculture Act, which would be redesignated Section 18. This section specifies that "nothing in this Act shall be construed to amend, repeal, or otherwise modify the authority of any Federal officer, department, or agency to perform any function, responsibility, or activity authorized under any other provision of law." The Department concurs with this provision.

The bill would establish the Secretary of Agriculture, in consultation with the Secretaries of Commerce and the Interior, and other Federal agency heads, to coordinate and implement a national policy for private aquaculture and to modify and update the National Aquaculture Development Plan. The Department concurs that the Secretary should provide leadership in the development, coordination, and implementation of a national policy for private, commercial aquaculture. However, given the important roles played by other agencies, we recommend that proposed new Section 8 (a) of the National Aquaculture Act be amended so that this policy is developed "in **coordination**", rather than "in consultation", with other Federal agencies.

The Department also recognizes that the National Aquaculture Development Plan addresses both private and public aquaculture. Consequently, the proposed amendment to Section 4 of the National Aquaculture Act and the proposed new Section 8 (c) should be revised to indicate that the Secretary, in **collaboration** with the Secretaries of Commerce and the Interior, and the heads of other agencies, as appropriate, shall revise the Plan. In addition, we object to the proposed new Section 8 (e) of the National Aquaculture Act, which specifies that the Secretary shall be responsible for resolving any interagency conflict. This provision would infringe upon the discretion of the Executive Branch to resolve interagency issues.

The bill would continue authorization for the National Aquaculture Information Center and would expand its responsibilities. The Center is an important resource for the U.S. aquaculture community and for the JSA.

The bill would authorize the Secretary to develop and implement an aquaculture commercialization program. The Department agrees that there is a need to support activities that can accelerate the transfer to the marketplace of promising aquaculture research and technologies.

Section 9 of the bill would authorize development of a program by the Administrator of the Environmental Protection Agency, in collaboration with the Secretary of Agriculture, to carry out collaborative, interagency programs that demonstrate the application of aquaculture to environmental enhancement and assessment. The Department supports programs that can demonstrate the compatibility of agricultural activities, including aquaculture, with responsible environmental stewardship. The Department recommends that this section be amended so that these programs are also carried out in collaboration with the Secretaries of Commerce and the Interior, and heads of other agencies, as appropriate.

The Department of Agriculture finds that the proposed legislation would apply broadly to the U.S. aquaculture industry, and would strengthen the Department's ability to support cultivation of a wide variety of aquatic species in diverse freshwater and marine environments throughout the United States. The legislation should be an important stimulus to the development of a globally competitive U.S. aquaculture industry. The Department welcomes the opportunity to provide needed assistance to this important developing industry.

These are only some of the issues that should be addressed before the Committee acts on this legislation. The Departments of Commerce and the Interior, as well as other agencies, will want to examine this bill more closely before they can comment.

Mr. Chairman, this concludes my prepared statement. I will be pleased to respond to any questions.

Statement of
Joseph P. McCraren, Executive Director
National Aquaculture Association
Before a Joint Hearing of the
Subcommittees on Department Operations and Nutrition
and Livestock
United States House of Representatives
October 4, 1994

RE: H.R. 4744, National Aquaculture Development, Commercialization, and Promotion Act of 1994

Thank you very much. Good afternoon Mr. Chairman and committee members. I am Joseph McCraren, Executive Director of the National Aquaculture Association. I wish to thank you for providing me personally, my colleagues, and our industry with the opportunity to speak in support of House Bill 4744, the National Aquaculture Development, Commercialization, and Promotion Act of 1994.

Today, I am speaking on behalf of all members of the National Aquaculture Association. NAA is the youngest and largest aquaculture association in the United States. It is a grass roots, producer-driven, non-profit organization dedicated to the establishment of policies that further the common interest of its membership, both as individual producers and as members of an industry. NAA currently serves 35 diverse national and state associations whose members produce a variety of species including trout, salmon, catfish, ornamentals and shellfish.

An analysis by the U.S. Department of Agriculture reveals that aquaculture production in 1980 was 203 million pounds with a farm gate value of $192 million. During the 1980's, production quadrupled reaching an estimated 860 million pounds, with a farm gate value of more than $760 million by 1990. Aquaculture is a growth industry as evidenced by these data.

Our nation's aquaculture producers range in size and complexity from corporations employing several hundred workers to small, family-owned farms, commonly referred to as "Mom and Pop" operations. They farm a variety of finfish, crustaceans, such as crawfish and shrimp, shellfish and aquatic plants. The industry is supported by an infrastructure of feed mills, processing plants, equipment manufacturers and suppliers. The United States industry and its support services account for nearly 300,000 full-time jobs, with a direct and indirect economic impact of $8 billion. And too, aquaculture supplies substantial quantities of finfish for the recreational fishery.

The potential for this industry, the fastest growing segment of agriculture in this country, is vast. Growth would mean jobs and opportunity to many Americans, particularly to those in our rural areas. It would provide farmers involved in traditional agriculture with a viable alternative.

Aquaculture currently accounts for less than 9 percent of U.S. seafood production compared to the world average of 16 percent. In 1990 the United States ranked 10th in world aquaculture production.

Aquaculture will be a major global growth industry of the 21st century. According to current projections, based on anticipated population growth and stable or declining capture fisheries harvest, aquaculture production will have to increase seven-fold to supply the world's demand for seafood by the year 2025. With national commitment and proper planning and support, the United States can realize a major opportunity to develop an important new agricultural industry to serve national needs and the global marketplace. Without such a commitment, the U.S. will continue to depend on imported fish and shellfish which now supply over 60 percent of our seafood needs. Fisheries imports--some $9 billion annually--constitute the third largest component of the U.S. trade deficit, after petroleum and automobiles. Realization of this legislation will contribute significantly and dramatically to the future of our industry and its meaningfulness to our economy.

We appreciate the fact that the Bill is of value to all segments of the industry and that it addresses a litany of rudimentary needs necessary for this industry's future. These include reauthorization of the National Aquaculture Act of 1980; provision for the coordination and implementation of a national aquaculture policy for private industry by the Secretary of Agriculture in consultation with the Secretaries of Commerce and Interior and others as appropriate. We support USDA as lead agency, since aquaculture is recognized as agriculture worldwide and should be viewed no differently in our Nation.

Further, cultured aquatic plants and animals would be treated as livestock and agricultural commodities. This is important as it relates to programs of the Department of Agriculture and industry. Important, as well, is reference to a Departmental aquaculture plan. We need a Departmental focus and infrastructure sensitive to this industry, with a budget reflective of its needs.

We applaud the innovative section on aquaculture commercialization research, revision of the National Aquaculture Development Plan, the Bill's facilitation of improved communication and interaction between private industry, Federal government and others who make up this diverse community. We are pleased, as well, with the all-inclusive reference to disaster assistance and certainly the opportunities that farm credit assistance would provide.

It is our hope that we have conveyed in these few minutes the need for this legislation to the subcommittees. We need this Bill; we urge House members to support its passage.

Our sincere thanks to the Subcommittees for agreeing to hold this hearing and to Congresswoman Lambert, her staff, and the original co-sponsors for developing and introducing this valuable legislation. I would be pleased to respond to any questions you might have.

(206) 273-5890 • FAX (206) 273-6577

WASHINGTON FISH GROWERS

10420 173rd Ave. SW • Rochester, WA 98579

TESTIMONY
SUPPORTING H.R. 4744
"THE NATIONAL AQUACULTURE DEVELOPMENT,
COMMERCIALIZATION, AND PROMOTION ACT"
BEFORE THE
'HOUSE SUBCOMMITTEE ON LIVESTOCK'
CHAIRMAN
CONGRESSMAN CHARLES W. STENHOLM
BY
JAMES R. ZIMMERMAN

Congressman Stenholm and members of the House Subcommittee on Livestock: My name is James R. Zimmerman, I am Director of Public Relations of Troutlodge, Inc. with offices in Sumner, Washington. I am here representing the Washington Fish Growers Association with 60 members in the Evergreen State of Washington active in farming of trout and salmon. Total production of trout, salmon and live eggs is nearing an annual farm gate value of $44 million. My parent company, Troutlodge, Inc., is the world's largest producer and supplier of live eyed rainbow trout eggs; shipping over 300 million eggs into 25 foreign countries and up to 30 States of the Union.

The Washington Fish Growers appreciates Congresswoman Lambert's sponsorship of H.R. 4744, an important Act for the aquatic farmers of America.

Mr. Chairman and members of the committee, we strongly support H.R. 4744. This legislation is important to aquatic farmers and it will facilitate a healthy growth in aquaculture and provide the following:

(A.) H.R. 4744 requires the Secretary of Agriculture to treat private aquaculture "as a form of agriculture" and aquaculture products moving in "standard commodity channels as agricultural commodities" and defining aquatic animals as "livestock". All of these definitions are absolutely critical to the advancement of aquaculture farming in America.

For example, with these definitions, it would be made clear that the USDA (through APHIS) could perform certification services for fish and live fish eggs as it currently does for other forms of agricultural livestock. NOTICE: For fish or live fish eggs to move intrastate, interstate or internationally, they must be "certified" free of listed diseases of the receiving state or nation.

In the past, aquatic farmers relied on the U.S. Fish and Wildlife Service for certification services. However, the availability of these services has been inconsistent, at best, and the services are presently unavailable in large parts of the country. USDA (APHIS) is recognized throughout the world for its certification of livestock. Certification by the USDA will be advantageous for firms who export fish products, such as live fish eggs & smolts.

(B.) H.R. 4744 recognizes the USDA as the lead agency in regulating and assisting in the expanding development of private sector aquaculture. Again, bringing aquaculture farming into mainstream agriculture is critical to future growth and success.

With the passage and signing into law of H.R. 4744, America will have more growing aquaculture farms. The following are additional benefits of H.R. 4744:

a. Presently America imports 60% of it's fish and fish products. A great deal of that could be grown in the United States. With a clear aquatic farming policy, lead by the USDA, American aquaculture could grow and increase exports, which will have a positive impact on the present trade imbalance.

b. Creation of employment opportunities in rural areas where jobs are most needed.

c. Increase American farming production of fish and fish products, thus, providing a consistent supply at competitive prices

The Washington Fish Growers Association strongly supports H.R. 4744 and we urge final passage.

We, again, extend our appreciation to Congresswomen Lambert for her leadership in sponsoring this very important legislation. We further extend our appreciation to the co-sponsors and respective members of the staff that have been very professional in assisting in the development of this aquaculture farming bill.

We again urge passage of H.R. 4744 and are prepared to address questions and lend assistance for support of House Resolution 4744.

Respectfully submitted by,

Jim Zimmerman

James R. Zimmerman
Troutlodge, Inc. - Director of Public Relations
Washington Fish Growers Asso. - Legislative Chairman

NATIONAL AQUACULTURE COUNCIL

A DIVISION OF
NATIONAL FISHERIES INSTITUTE

1525 WILSON BOULEVARD • SUITE 500 • ARLINGTON, VA 22209 • (703) 524-8883 • FAX (703) 524-4619

TESTIMONY OF THE NATIONAL AQUACULTURE COUNCIL IN SUPPORT OF HOUSE BILL HR-4744: "THE NATIONAL AQUACULTURE DEVELOPMENT COMMERCIALIZATION, AND PROMOTION ACT OF 1994"

I WOULD LIKE TO TAKE THIS OPPORTUNITY TO THANK CONGRESSMAN STENHOLM AND MEMBERS OF BOTH THE HOUSE AGRICULTURE SUBCOMMITTEE ON DEPARTMENT OPERATIONS AND NUTRITION AND THE SUBCOMMITTEE ON LIVESTOCK FOR THE INVITATION TO ADDRESS THIS MOST IMPORTANT PIECE OF LEGISLATIVE.

MY NAME IS ROY MARTIN, I AM THE EXECUTIVE DIRECTOR OF THE NATIONAL AQUACULTURE COUNCIL AND VICE PRESIDENT OF THE NATIONAL FISHERIES INSTITUTE. THE COUNCIL AND INSTITUTE REPRESENT OVER 1,000 COMPANIES ENGAGED IN ALL THE MANY ASPECTS OF SEAFOOD PRODUCTION, MARKETING AND DISTRIBUTION.

WE SINCERELY APPRECIATE CONGRESSWOMAN LAMBERT'S INTEREST

TESTIMONY OF THE NATIONAL AQUACULTURE COUNCIL IN SUPPORT OF HOUSE BILL HR-4744: "THE NATIONAL AQUACULTURE DEVELOPMENT COMMERCIALIZATION, AND PROMOTION ACT OF 1994"

IN THE U.S. AQUACULTURE INDUSTRY AND THE DEVELOPMENT OF HR-4744.

THE NATIONAL AQUACULTURE COUNCIL FULLY SUPPORTS THE INTENT OF HR-4744. THE COUNCIL AGREES THAT AQUACULTURE NEEDS THE SUPPORT OF THE ELEMENTS CONTAINED IN THIS BILL.

THIS WHOLE SUBJECT IS SOMETHING THAT GOES BEYOND COMMITTEE JURISDICTION. THIS IS AN ISSUE FOR THE COUNTRY.

IF THE CONGRESS AND THE ADMINISTRATION ARE REALLY SERIOUS ABOUT AQUACULTURE, AND I BELIEVE THE CONGRESS IS, THEN THE FOLLOWING FACTS AND NEEDS SHOULD NOT BE DENIED:

TO NO ONES SURPRISE THE PRIVATE AQUACULTURE INDUSTRY IS DIVERSE, BUT GROWING FASTER THAN ANY OTHER SEGMENT OF AGRICULTURE. THAT'S A GREAT START. WE NOW ESTIMATE THAT WE EMPLOY 300,000 IN ACTUAL AND RELATED JOBS. WHAT KIND OF JOBS-RURAL JOBS. THAT'S ANOTHER POSITIVE.

TESTIMONY OF THE NATIONAL AQUACULTURE COUNCIL IN SUPPORT OF HOUSE BILL HR-4744: "THE NATIONAL AQUACULTURE DEVELOPMENT COMMERCIALIZATION, AND PROMOTION ACT OF 1994"

U.S. POPULATION ROSE AGAIN LAST YEAR BUT SO DID TOTAL U.S. CONSUMPTION OF SEAFOOD. WILD STOCKS ARE ON A DECLINE, THEY NEED A REST, WHAT WILL FILL THE CONTINUED DEMAND?------AQUACULTURE COULD WITH PROPER SUPPORT. NO ONE QUESTIONS THE NEED FOR THE NUTRITIONAL BENEFITS THAT ACCOMPANY CONSUMPTION OF SEAFOOD.

WE ARE THE FIRST PROTECTORS OF WATER QUALITY NOT EPA.

WE NEED AN AQUACULTURE POLICY FOR THE U.S.

WHERE DOES THE LEADERSHIP REALLY STAND ON THIS ISSUE? AQUACULTURE NO MATTER HOW YOU DEFINE IT IS HUSBANDRY, FARMING, RANCHING, LIVESTOCK, ANIMAL HEALTH---IN OTHER WORDS AGRICULTURE.

THE WORD AQUACULTURE NEEDS A LEADER, A LEADER THAT CAN COORDINATE ITS VARIOUS INTERPRETATIONS BY OTHER COMMITTEES AND DEPARTMENTS OF GOVERNMENT---USDA IS THAT LEADER. TO MAINTAIN THIS PATTERN OF GROWTH WE WILL NEED A HIGHLY FOCUSED RESEARCH,

DEVELOPMENT, AND TECHNOLOGY TRANSFER PROGRAM---ALL THE ELEMENTS THAT ARE INCLUDED IN THIS LEGISLATION.

WE HAVE A NATIONAL RESOURCE THAT IS BEGGING FOR SUPPORT, THE AQUACULTURE LIBRARY.

WE MUST SUPPORT THE EDUCATIONAL ASPECTS OF THIS BILL. WITHOUT THE AIC SUPPORT EDUCATIONAL INFORMATION WILL NOT BE READILY AVAILABLE FOR OUR FUTURE GENERATIONS OF AQUACULTURISTS OR BUSINESS LEADERS IN THE AGRICULTURE COMMUNITY.

DISASTER ASSISTANCE IS A NEEDED PART OF THIS BILL AND WE SUPPORT IT.

AS I'VE SAID IN SENATE TESTIMONY, I AM STRUCK BY THE OPPORTUNITIES GIVEN TO JOBS AND RURAL DEVELOPMENT BY THIS INDUSTRY AS I TRAVEL THE FARMS, PROCESSING PLANTS AND SMALL

TESTIMONY OF THE NATIONAL AQUACULTURE COUNCIL IN SUPPORT OF HOUSE BILL HR-4744: "THE NATIONAL AQUACULTURE DEVELOPMENT COMMERCIALIZATION, AND PROMOTION ACT OF 1994"

TOWNS AND MEET THE DOWN HOME FOLKS THAT ARE U.S. AQUACULTURE.

WE NEED ACTION NOT MORE WORDS.

IN CLOSING, I WOULD LIKE TO THANK THE COMMITTEES FOR THIS OPPORTUNITY TO PRESENT OUR VIEWS ON HR-4744.

Dear Chairman Stenholm and other honorable members of the House Agriculture Subcommittee on Department Operations and Nutrition and the House Agriculture Subcommittee on Livestock:

I am Carlton Dorey of Brightwater Farms from Arkansas' First Congressional District. I am a catfish farmer and processor who would like to testify to you concerning the importance of the "National Aquaculture Development, Commercialization, and Promotion Act of 1994" (H.R. 4744) to my industry.

This bill establishes USDA as the lead agency for aquaculture which I feel is the correct thing to do because after all: Aquaculture is Agriculture. With USDA as our lead agency, the aquaculture industry will be able to secure a national policy for aquaculture instead of a national strategy. This will enable aquaculture to be included and recognized in all federal farm programs. My industry is not looking for special treatment by the federal government, we just want to be treated the same as other farmers. Natural disasters strike our farms too and fish farmers should be eligible for farm credit loans and disaster assistance.

This bill states that the Secretary of Agriculture will be the permanent chairperson of the Joint Subcommittee on Aquaculture. Currently this chair is rotated between the Secretaries of Agriculture, Commerce, and Interior. It is imperative that the Secretary of Agriculture permanently chair this subcommittee to insure continuity in our national aquaculture policy. We are like a ship with three captains that all want to steer us to a different "policy" port. The aquaculture industry in the United States needs a sense of direction from the federal government. Our industry will continue to be regulated by numerous federal agencies but we need a single agency for guidance and assistance.

As a young industry, our research needs are great and our research dollars are limited. This bill will coordinate our research efforts so that these limited dollars will not be wasted on duplicated research.

I know that other aquaculture bills have been introduced into the House of Representatives but this bill has truly been written with industry input and only it addresses the issue of a single lead agency.

As you have heard many times, aquaculture is one of the fastest growing segments of the agriculture economy even with our current fragmented national strategy. Just think of our potential growth and ability to help reduce the national balance-of-payment deficit once this bill is enacted. Aquaculture is providing job opportunities in our rural areas and is providing an area of diversification for existing traditional farms that will enable them to be more profitable.

This is a good bill, it has wide industry support, and I urge you to act favorably upon.

STATEMENT OF THE AMERICAN FARM BUREAU FEDERATION TO THE HOUSE AGRICULTURE SUBCOMMITTEE ON DEPARTMENT OPERATIONS AND NUTRITION, AND THE HOUSE SUBCOMMITTEE ON LIVESTOCK REGARDING H.R. 4744, THE NATIONAL AQUACULTURE DEVELOPMENT, COMMERCIALIZATION AND PROMOTION ACT OF 1994.

October 4, 1994

The American Farm Bureau Federation (AFBF), the largest general farm organization in the United States with over four million member families, appreciates the opportunity to comment on H.R. 4744, the National Aquaculture Development, Commercialization, and Promotion Act of 1994.

AFBF applauds the efforts of Congresswoman Lambert and Chairman de la Garza in focusing attention on the aquaculture industry. We hope their efforts will be the catalyst for a significant increase in interest by the House Agriculture Committee in aquaculture.

The aquaculture industry in the United States is diverse and growing rapidly. With production increasing five-fold during the 1980's, aquaculture is now the fastest growing sector of American agriculture. Farmgate receipts now exceed $800 million yearly. This creates an economic impact of over $8 billion with nearly 300,000 aquaculture-related jobs.

Demand for seafood is rising steadily. Per capita consumption in the United States grew 20 percent a year in the 1980's. Doubling of domestic consumption is projected by the year 2020. Will this demand be met by domestic production or imports? America's annual trade deficit in fisheries products has been $4.5 to $7.0 billion since 1987. This trade imbalance is the largest of any agricultural commodity and second only to petroleum among natural products.

The nutritional benefits of seafood are well-known and are contributing to aquaculture's growth.

Aquaculture can be an integral component of economic development plans while preserving environmental quality. Commercial success of an operation requires clean water supplies and maintenance of superior water quality. Aquaculture can also convert non-productive land areas into economic and recreational assets. An example is the reclamation of abandoned mine pits.

AFBF not only supports H.R. 4744 for the aforementioned reasons but also because it:

*Declares a national aquaculture policy. A coordinated and supportive federal policy can help overcome constraints to aquaculture development in the United States.

*Establishes aquaculture as a form of agriculture. Aquaculture has developed as a solid alternative agricultural opportunity and has allowed traditional farmers to diversify. The development of modern aquaculture can be compared with the much earlier changes in livestock production, away from the hunting of wild animals and toward the animal husbandry that exists today. Aquaculture development programs will benefit by being considered in the context of total farm profitability and by being integrated with traditional agriculture.

*Establishes the U.S. Department of Agriculture (USDA) as the lead federal agency. USDA has been designated by Congress as the lead agency for the coordination of aquacultural activities at the federal level. Despite this mandate, however, USDA has not exercised effective control. Within the department, aquaculture activities occur in 14 different agencies. Outside the department, aquaculture activities are found in the Department of Commerce (Sea Grant and National Marine Fisheries Service) and the Department of the Interior (U.S. Fish and Wildlife Service). By reaffirming USDA's leadership role in aquaculture, the development of the aquaculture industry will be enhanced.

The bill's focus on commercialization of research is also important. AFBF supports effective research which has an immediate positive economic impact, but it should not be forgotten that the need for basic research is essential since it is really the basis for applied research.

Disaster assistance for aquaculture is appropriate. It is important that the structure of the program be based on realistic assumptions about possible monetary losses.

The American Farm Bureau Federation supports the passage of H.R. 4744.

○